CW00369072

SOUPS &
STARTERS

Published by Hinkler Books Pty Ltd
45–55 Fairchild Street
Heatherton Victoria 3202 Australia
www.hinkler.com.au

hinkler

Prepress: Splitting Image
Typesetting: MPS Ltd
Design: Pandemonium Creative
© A.C.N. 144 619 894 Pty Ltd 2011

ISBN: 978 1 7418 4098 8

Printed and bound in China

CONTENTS

INTRODUCTION

When you are planning a menu, whether it is for a dinner party, a casual barbecue or a weeknight family meal, you should always aim to make it as delicious and enjoyable as possible. It is important to contrast flavours, textures and ingredients.

Starters should complement the rest of your meal and be planned keeping in mind the dishes being served for the rest of the meal.

Soups are a perfect start to a meal. The more substantial soups are sufficient to make a meal in themselves and are a versatile way of using the freshest ingredients of every category of food. The basis of a good soup is a good-quality stock (broth) and the best way to achieve that is to make your own.

The type of soup or starter you serve will depend on the occasion, the number of guests and even the weather. *Pocket Chef Soups & Starters* offers a wide range of appetising options to begin many different kinds of meals.

CHEESE CRACKERS

Preparation time:
10 minutes + 1 hour refrigeration

Total cooking time:
15 minutes

Makes about 60

INGREDIENTS

- 1 cup (125 g/4⅓ oz) plain
  (all-purpose) flour
- 2 tablespoons self-raising flour
- 1 teaspoon curry powder
- 125 g (4⅓) butter
- ½ cup (50 g/1¾ oz)
  grated Parmesan
- ⅔ cup (85 g/3 oz) grated Cheddar
  (American) cheese
- 20 g (⅔ oz) crumbled
  blue-vein cheese
- 1 tablespoon lemon juice
- ¼ cup (25 g/¾ oz) finely grated
  Parmesan, extra

1 Place the flours, curry powder
  and butter in a food processor.
  Process until the mixture
  resembles fine breadcrumbs.

2 Stir in the cheeses and the lemon
  juice. Bring the mixture together
  into a ball.

3 Roll into a 30 cm (12 inch) log.
  Wrap in plastic wrap and chill for
  1 hour. Slice into 5 mm (¼ inch)
  slices. Reshape if necessary.
  Preheat the oven to moderately
  hot 200°C (400°F/Gas 6).

4 Place on a baking paper-lined
  oven tray (sheet), allowing some
  room for spreading. Sprinkle
  the tops with Parmesan. Bake
  for 15 minutes, or until the
  crackers are golden. Cool on
  the trays (sheets).

SPINACH DIP

Preparation time:
10 minutes + 3 hours refrigeration

Total cooking time:
Nil

Serves 6–8

INGREDIENTS

- 250 g (8¾ oz) frozen chopped spinach
- 300 g (10½ oz) ricotta
- ¾ cup (185 g/6½ oz) sour cream
- 30 g (1 oz) packet spring vegetable soup mix
- 4 spring (green) onions, finely chopped

1 Thaw the spinach and squeeze out as much liquid as possible with your hands.

2 Process the spinach, ricotta, sour cream, soup mix and spring (green) onions in a food processor or blender until smooth. Cover and refrigerate for 2–3 hours. Serve with crisp lavash bread, crackers or assorted crisp vegetables such as blanched snow peas (mange tout), cauliflower and carrots.

NOTE: Can be made a week in advance.

TAPENADE

Preparation time:
10 minutes

Total cooking time:
Nil

Makes 1½ cups

INGREDIENTS

- 400 g (14 oz) Kalamata olives, pitted
- 2 cloves garlic, crushed
- 2 anchovy fillets in oil, drained
- 2 tablespoons capers in brine,
  rinsed, squeezed dry
- 2 teaspoons chopped fresh thyme
- 2 teaspoons Dijon mustard
- 1 tablespoon lemon juice
- ¼ cup (60 ml/2 fl oz) olive oil
- 1 tablespoon brandy, optional

1 Process all the ingredients together in a food processor until they form a smooth consistency. Season with freshly ground black pepper. Spoon into a sterilised, warm jar (see NOTE), seal and refrigerate for up to 2 weeks.

NOTE: To prepare a sterilised storage jar, preheat the oven to very slow 120°C (250°F/Gas ½). Wash the jar and lid in hot soapy water and rinse with hot water. Put the jar in the oven for 20 minutes, or until fully dry. Do not dry with a tea towel. If refrigerated, the olive oil may solidify, making it white. This will not affect the flavour of the dish. Bring to room temperature before serving and the oil will return to a liquid state.

SMOKED TROUT DIP

Preparation time:
25 minutes

Total cooking time:
Nil

Serves 4–6

INGREDIENTS

- 250 g (8¾ oz) smoked rainbow trout
- 1½ teaspoons olive oil
- ½ cup (125 ml/4¼ fl oz) cream
- 1 tablespoon lemon juice
- pinch of cayenne (red) pepper

1 Remove the skin and bones from the smoked trout. Put the flesh in a food processor or blender with the olive oil, 2 teaspoons of the cream and the lemon juice. Blend to a thick paste, then slowly add the remaining cream until well mixed. Season, to taste, with salt and the cayenne (red) pepper. Serve with grissini or water crackers and baby radishes or other vegetables, for dipping.

NOTE: This dip can be made a few days ahead and kept, covered, in the refrigerator.

CHEESE AND CHILLI SHAPES

Preparation time:
10 minutes + 30 minutes refrigeration

Total cooking time:
20 minutes

Makes 12

INGREDIENTS

- 1¼ cups (155 g/5½ oz) plain (all-purpose) flour
- pinch dry hot mustard
- 90 g (3¼ oz) butter, roughly chopped
- ½ cup (60 g/2 oz) grated vintage Cheddar (American) cheese
- 4 red chillies, seeded and sliced
- 1 egg yolk

1 Process the flour, mustard and butter until they resemble fine breadcrumbs. Add the cheese and chilli, then the egg yolk and 1 tablespoon water, and process until the mixture comes together. Gather into a ball, cover with plastic wrap and refrigerate for 30 minutes.

2 Preheat the oven to 190°C (375°F/Gas 5). On a lightly floured surface, roll out the dough to a 5 mm (¼ inch) thickness. Cut into 5 cm (2 inch) rounds.

3 Place on lightly greased baking trays (sheets) and bake for 15–20 minutes, or until golden. Cool.

TARAMOSALATA

Preparation time:
10 minutes + soaking

Total cooking time:
Nil

Makes 1½ cups

INGREDIENTS

* 5 slices white bread,
  crusts removed
* ⅓ cup (80 ml/2¾ fl oz) milk
* 100 g (3½ oz) can tarama
  (grey mullet roe)
* 1 egg yolk
* ½ small onion, grated
* 1 clove garlic, crushed
* 2 tablespoons lemon juice
* ⅓ cup (80 ml/2¾ fl oz) olive oil
* pinch of ground white pepper

1 Soak the bread in the milk for
  10 minutes. Press in a strainer to
  extract excess milk, then mix in
  a food processor with the tarama,
  egg yolk, onion and garlic for
  30 seconds, or until smooth.
  Mix in 1 tablespoon lemon juice.

2 With the motor running, slowly
  pour in the olive oil. The mixture
  should be smooth. Add the
  remaining lemon juice and white
  pepper. If the dip tastes too salty,
  add another piece of bread.

NOTE: Grey mullet roe is
traditional but smoked cod's roe
also gives a lovely flavour.

HUMMUS

Preparation time:
20 minutes + overnight soaking

Total cooking time:
1 hour 15 minutes

Makes 3 cups

INGREDIENTS

* 1 cup (220 g/7¾ oz) dried
  chickpeas (garbanzo beans)
* 2 tablespoons tahini
* 4 cloves garlic, crushed
* 2 teaspoons ground cumin
* ⅓ cup (80 ml/2¾ fl oz) lemon juice
* 3 tablespoons olive oil
* large pinch of cayenne (red) pepper
* extra lemon juice, optional
* extra virgin olive oil, to garnish
* paprika, to garnish
* chopped fresh flat-leaf parsley,
  to garnish

1 Put the chickpeas (garbanzo
   beans) in a bowl, add 1 litre
   (1.1 US qt/1.75 UK pt) water,
   then soak overnight. Drain and
   place in a large saucepan with
   2 litres (2.1 US qt/1.75 UK qt)
   water, or enough to cover the

chickpeas (garbanzo beans) by
5 cm (2 inches). Bring to the
boil, then reduce the heat and
simmer for 1 hour 15 minutes,
or until the chickpeas (garbanzo
beans) are very tender. Skim any
scum from the surface. Drain
well, reserving the cooking liquid
and leave until cool enough to
handle. Pick through for any
loose skins and discard them.

2 Combine the chickpeas
   (garbanzo beans), tahini, garlic,
   cumin, lemon juice, olive oil,
   cayenne (red) pepper and
   1½ teaspoons salt in a food
   processor until thick and smooth.
   With the motor running,
   gradually add enough of the
   reserved cooking liquid, about
   ¾ cup (185 ml/6½ fl oz), to
   form a smooth creamy puree.
   Season with salt or some extra
   lemon juice.

3 Spread onto flat bowls or plates,
   drizzle with the extra virgin olive
   oil, sprinkle with paprika and
   scatter parsley over the top.
   Delicious served with warm pita
   bread or pide.

PANISSES

Preparation time:
20 minutes + cooling

Total cooking time:
30 minutes

Serves 6

INGREDIENTS

- 170 g (6 oz) chickpea (garbanzo bean) flour
- 1½ tablespoons olive oil
- vegetable oil, for frying

1 Spray six saucers with cooking oil spray. Place the flour in a bowl and stir in 2¾ cups (685 ml/ 24 fl oz) cold water. Whisk with a wire whisk for about 2 minutes, or until smooth. Stir in the olive oil and season, to taste, with salt and finely ground black pepper.

2 Pour into a heavy-based saucepan and cook over low heat for about 8 minutes, stirring constantly, until thickened. Cook and stir until the mixture goes lumpy and starts to pull away from the sides of the pan, about 10–12 minutes.

Remove from the heat and beat until smooth. Working quickly before the mixture sets, distribute among the saucers and spread to an even thickness. Allow to cool and set.

3 Preheat the oven to very slow 120°C (250°F/Gas ½). Remove the mixture from the saucers and cut into sticks 5 cm (2 inches) long and 2 cm (¾ inch) wide. Pour vegetable oil into a large heavy-based saucepan to a depth of about 2.5 cm (1 inch). Heat to very hot and fry the sticks in batches until crisp and golden, about 2 minutes on each side. Remove with a slotted spoon and drain on crumpled paper towels. Transfer cooked batches to trays (sheets) and keep warm in the oven while the rest are being fried. Serve hot, sprinkled with salt and freshly ground black pepper and perhaps some grated Parmesan.

NOTE: For a sweet snack, sprinkle with sugar while still hot.

CHILLI CRAB AND TOMATO DIP

Preparation time:	**Total cooking time:**	**Serves** 6
25 minutes	Nil	

INGREDIENTS

- 1 small ripe tomato
- 2 × 170 g (6 oz) cans crab meat, drained
- 200 g (7 oz) neufchatel cheese (see NOTE)
- 2 tablespoons chilli (pepper) sauce

- 2 teaspoons tomato paste (tomato puree)
- 1 teaspoon grated lemon rind
- 2 teaspoons lemon juice
- 1 small onion, finely grated
- 2 spring (green) onions, finely sliced

1 Score a cross in the base of the tomato. Place in a heatproof bowl and cover with boiling water. Leave for 30 seconds, transfer to cold water, drain and peel away from the cross. Cut the tomato in half, scoop out the seeds with a teaspoon and finely chop the flesh.

2 Squeeze any liquid from the crab meat with your hands. Beat the neufchatel in a bowl with a wooden spoon until smooth, then stir in the crab meat, chilli (pepper) sauce, tomato paste (tomato puree), lemon rind, lemon juice and grated onion.

Season well with salt and pepper. Mix together and spoon into a serving bowl.

3 Scatter the sliced spring (green) onion and chopped tomato over the top. Refrigerate, covered, before serving. Can be served with thinly sliced or lightly toasted bread. A small serving spoon makes it easier for guests.

NOTE: Neufchatel is a smooth, mild, good-quality cream cheese available from delicatessens. If it is not available, another cream cheese can be used instead.

MARINATED ROASTED VEGETABLE DIP

Preparation time:
55 minutes + marinating

Total cooking time:
50 minutes

Serves 8

INGREDIENTS

* 1 small eggplant (aubergine), sliced
* 2 zucchini (courgettes), sliced
* 3 red capsicums (peppers)
* ½ cup (125 ml/4¼ fl oz) extra virgin olive oil
* 2 cloves garlic, sliced
* 2 Roma tomatoes
* 200 g (7 oz) canned artichoke hearts, drained
* 7 g (¼ oz) fresh oregano leaves
* 250 g (8¾ oz) ricotta cheese
* 45 g (1⅔ oz) black (ripe) olives, pitted and sliced

1 Place the eggplant (aubergine) and zucchini (courgette) in a colander over a bowl, sprinkle generously with salt and leave for 15–20 minutes. Meanwhile, cut the red capsicums (peppers) into large flat pieces, removing the seeds and membrane. Cook, skin-side-up, under a hot grill (broiler) until the skin is black and blistered. Cool in a plastic bag, then peel. Reserve about a quarter of the capsicums (peppers) to use as a garnish and place the rest in a large non-metallic bowl.

2 Place half the olive oil in a bowl, add 1 garlic clove and a pinch of salt and mix. Rinse the eggplant (aubergine) and zucchini (courgette) and pat dry with paper towels. Place the eggplant (aubergine) on a non-stick or foil-lined tray (sheet) and brush with the garlic oil. Cook under a very hot grill (broiler) for 4–6 minutes each side, or until golden brown, brushing both sides with oil during grilling (broiling). The eggplant (aubergine) will burn easily, so keep a close watch. Allow to cool while grilling (broiling) the zucchini (courgette) in the same way. Add both to the red capsicum (pepper) in the bowl.

3 Slice the tomatoes lengthways, place on a non-stick or foil-lined baking tray (sheet) and brush with the garlic oil. Reduce the temperature slightly and grill (broil) for 10–15 minutes, or until soft. Add to the bowl with the other vegetables.

4 Cut the artichokes into quarters and add to the bowl. Mix in any remaining garlic oil along with the remaining olive oil. Stir in the oregano and remaining garlic. Cover with a tight-fitting lid or plastic wrap and refrigerate for at least 2 hours.

5 Drain the vegetables and place in a food processor. Add the ricotta and process for 20 seconds, or until smooth. Reserve a tablespoon of olives to garnish. Add the rest to the processor. Mix in a couple of short bursts, then transfer to a non-metallic bowl and cover with plastic wrap. Chill for at least 2 hours.

6 Slice the reserved roasted red capsicum (pepper) into fine strips and arrange over the top of the dip with the reserved olives.

ARTICHOKE DIP

Preparation time:
10 minutes

Total cooking time:
15 minutes

Serves 8

INGREDIENTS

- 2 × 400 g (14 oz) cans artichoke hearts, drained
- 1 cup (250 g/8¾ oz) mayonnaise
- ¼ cup (75 g/2⅔ oz) grated Parmesan
- 2 teaspoons onion flakes
- 2 tablespoons grated Parmesan, extra
- paprika, to sprinkle

1 Preheat the oven to 180°C (350°F/Gas 4). Gently squeeze the artichokes to remove any remaining liquid. Chop and place in a bowl. Stir through the mayonnaise, Parmesan and the onion flakes.

2 Spread into a 1-litre (1.1 US qt/ 1.75 UK pt) capacity shallow ovenproof dish. Sprinkle with the extra Parmesan and a little paprika. Bake for 15 minutes, or until heated through and lightly browned on top. Serve with crusty bread.

GUACAMOLE

Preparation time:
30 minutes

Total cooking time:
Nil

Serves 6

INGREDIENTS

- 3 ripe avocados
- 1 tablespoon lime or lemon juice (see HINT)
- 1 tomato
- 1–2 red chillies, finely chopped
- 1 small red onion, finely chopped
- 1 tablespoon finely chopped fresh coriander (cilantro) leaves
- 2 tablespoons sour cream
- 1–2 drops hot chilli (pepper) sauce or habanero sauce

1 Roughly chop the avocado flesh and place in a bowl. Mash lightly with a fork and sprinkle with the lime or lemon juice to prevent the avocado discolouring.

2 Cut the tomato in half horizontally and use a teaspoon to scoop out the seeds. Finely dice the flesh and add to the avocado.

3 Stir in the chilli, onion, coriander (cilantro), sour cream and hot sauce. Season with freshly cracked black pepper.

4 Serve immediately or cover the surface with plastic wrap and refrigerate for 1–2 hours. If refrigerated, allow to come to room temperature before serving.

HINT: You will need 1–2 limes to produce 1 tablespoon of juice, depending on the lime. A heavier lime will probably be more juicy. To get more juice from a citrus fruit, prick it all over with a fork and then heat on High (100%) in the microwave for 1 minute. Don't forget to prick it or the fruit may burst.

CORNISH PASTIES

Preparation time:
1 hour + chilling
Total cooking time:
45 minutes
Makes 6

INGREDIENTS

- 2½ cups (310 g / 11 oz) plain (all-purpose) flour
- 125 g (4⅓ oz) butter, chilled and cubed
- 4–5 tablespoons iced water
- 160 g (5⅔ oz) rump (round or boneless sirloin steak) steak, diced
- 1 small potato, finely chopped
- 1 small onion, finely chopped
- 1 small carrot, finely chopped
- 1–2 teaspoons Worcestershire sauce
- 2 tablespoons beef stock (broth)
- 1 egg, lightly beaten

1 Grease a baking tray (sheet). Mix the flour, butter and a pinch of salt in a food processor for 15 seconds, or until crumbly. Add the water and process in short bursts until it comes together. Turn out onto a floured surface and form into a ball. Wrap in plastic and chill for 30 minutes. Preheat the oven to 210°C (415°F / Gas 6–7).

2 Mix together the steak, potato, onion, carrot, Worcestershire sauce and stock (broth). Season well.

3 Divide the dough into six portions and roll out to 3 mm (⅛ inch) thick. Cut into six 16 cm (6⅓ inch) rounds. Divide the filling evenly and put in the centre of each pastry circle.

4 Brush the pastry edges with egg and fold over. Pinch to form a frill and place on the tray (sheet). Brush with egg and bake for 15 minutes. Lower the heat to 180°C (350°F / Gas 4) and bake for 25–30 minutes, or until golden.

POTATO AND SALMON PARCELS

Preparation time:
30 minutes

Total cooking time:
40 minutes

Makes 12

INGREDIENTS

- 750 g (1 lb 10 oz) floury potatoes, peeled
- 40 g (1½ oz) butter
- ¼ cup (60 ml/2 fl oz) cream
- 1 cup (125 g/4⅓ oz) grated Cheddar (American) cheese
- 210 g (7⅓ oz) can red salmon, skin and bones removed, flaked
- 1 tablespoon chopped fresh dill (dill weed)
- 4 spring (green) onions, finely chopped
- 3 sheets puff pastry
- 1 egg, lightly beaten, to glaze

1 Cut the potatoes into small pieces and cook in a pan of boiling water until tender. Mash with the butter and the cream until there are no lumps. Lightly grease two oven trays (sheets).

2 Add the cheese, salmon, dill (dill weed) and spring (green) onion to the potato and mix well. Preheat the oven to 200°C (400°F/Gas 6). Cut each pastry sheet into four squares. Divide the mixture among the squares (approximately ¼ cup in each). Lightly brush the edges with beaten egg. Bring all four corners to the centre to form a point and press together to make a parcel.

3 Put the parcels on the greased trays (sheets) and glaze with egg. Bake for 15–20 minutes, or until the pastry is golden brown.

NOTE: Before removing the pastries from the oven, lift them gently off the tray (sheet) and check that the bottom of the parcels are cooked through. Take care not to overcook the parcels or they may burst open.

HINT: If you like your puff pastry to taste extra buttery, brush it with melted butter before baking.

SPINACH AND FETA TRIANGLES

Preparation time:
30 minutes

Total cooking time:
40 minutes

Makes 8

INGREDIENTS

- 1 kg (2 lb 3 oz) English (common) spinach (see VARIATION)
- ¼ cup (60 ml/2 fl oz) olive oil
- 1 onion, chopped
- 10 spring (green) onions, sliced
- ⅓ cup (20 g/⅔ oz) chopped fresh parsley
- 1 tablespoon chopped fresh dill (dill weed)
- large pinch of ground nutmeg
- ⅓ cup (35 g/1¼ oz) grated Parmesan
- 150 g (5¼ oz) crumbled feta
- 90 g (3¼ oz) ricotta
- 4 eggs, lightly beaten
- 40 g (1½ oz) butter, melted
- 1 tablespoon olive oil, extra
- 12 sheets filo (phyllo) pastry

1 Trim any coarse stems from the spinach. Wash the leaves thoroughly, roughly chop and place in a large pan with just a little water clinging to the leaves. Cover and cook gently over low heat for 5 minutes, or until the leaves have wilted. Drain well and allow to cool slightly before squeezing tightly to remove the excess water.

2 Heat the oil in a frying pan. Add the onion and cook over low heat for 10 minutes, or until soft and golden. Add the spring (green) onion and cook for a further 3 minutes. Remove from the heat. Stir in the drained spinach, parsley, dill (dill weed), nutmeg, Parmesan, feta, ricotta and egg. Season well.

3 Preheat the oven to 180°C (350°F/Gas 4). Grease two baking trays (sheets). Combine the melted butter with the extra oil. Work with three sheets of pastry at a time, keeping the rest covered with a damp tea towel. Brush each pastry sheet with butter mixture and lay them on top of each other. Cut in half lengthways.

4 Place 4 tablespoons of the filling on an angle at the end of each strip. Fold the pastry over to enclose the filling and form a triangle. Continue folding over until you reach the end of the pastry. Put on the baking trays (sheets) and brush with the remaining butter mixture. Bake for 20–25 minutes, or until the pastry is golden brown.

VARIATION: If you are unable to buy English (common) spinach, silverbeet (swiss chard) can be used instead. Use the same quantity and trim the coarse white stems from the leaves.

NOTE: Feta is a traditional Greek-style salty cheese. Any left over should be stored immersed in lightly salted water and kept refrigerated. Rinse and pat dry before using.

WONTON STACKS WITH TUNA AND GINGER

Preparation time:
20 minutes

Total cooking time:
10 minutes

Makes 24

INGREDIENTS

- 1½ tablespoons sesame seeds
- 12 fresh won ton wrappers
- ½ cup (125 ml/4¼ fl oz) peanut or vegetable oil
- 150 g (5¼ oz) piece fresh tuna fillet (see NOTE)
- ¼ cup (60 g/2 oz) Japanese mayonnaise
- 50 g (1¾ oz) pickled ginger (gingerroot)
- 50 g (1¾ oz) snow pea (mange tout) sprouts
- 2 teaspoons mirin
- 2 teaspoons soy sauce
- ¼ teaspoon sugar

1 Lightly toast the sesame seeds in a small dry frying pan over low heat for 2–3 minutes, or until golden.

2 Cut the won ton wrappers into quarters to give 48 squares in total. Heat the oil in a small saucepan over medium heat and cook the wrappers in batches for 1–2 minutes, or until they are golden and crisp. Drain on crumpled paper towels.

3 Thinly slice the tuna into 24 slices. Spoon approximately ¼ teaspoon of the mayonnaise onto 24 of the won ton squares. Place a slice of tuna on the mayonnaise and top with a little of the pickled ginger (gingerroot), snow pea (mange tout) sprouts and sesame seeds.

4 Mix the mirin, soy sauce and sugar together in a small bowl and drizzle a little over each stack. Season with pepper. Top with the remaining 24 won ton squares (lids). Serve immediately or the stacks will absorb the dressing and become soggy.

NOTE: For this recipe, you need good-quality tuna. Sashimi tuna is the best quality, but if you can't get that, buy only the freshest tuna with as little sinew as possible.

THINK AHEAD: The won ton wrappers can be fried the day before serving. Store them in an airtight container large enough that they are not cramped. Place sheets of paper towels between each layer.

TOFU TRIANGLES

Preparation time:
30 minutes + 4 hours refrigeration

Total cooking time:
20 minutes

Serves 4

INGREDIENTS

- 150 g (5¼ oz) firm tofu
- 2 spring (green) onions, chopped
- 3 teaspoons chopped fresh coriander (cilantro) leaves
- ½ teaspoon grated orange rind
- 2 teaspoons soy sauce
- 1 tablespoon sweet chilli sauce (jalapeno jelly)
- 2 teaspoons grated fresh ginger (gingerroot)
- 1 teaspoon cornflour (cornstarch)
- ½ cup (125 ml/4¼ fl oz) seasoned rice vinegar
- ¼ cup (60 g/2 oz) sugar
- 1 small Lebanese cucumber, finely diced
- 1 small red chilli, thinly sliced
- 1 spring (green) onion, extra, thinly sliced on the diagonal
- 2 sheets puff pastry
- 1 egg, lightly beaten

1 Drain the tofu, then pat dry and cut into small cubes.

2 Put the spring (green) onion, coriander (cilantro), rind, soy and chilli sauces, ginger (gingerroot), cornflour (cornstarch) and tofu in a bowl and gently mix. Cover, then refrigerate for 3–4 hours.

3 To make a dipping sauce, put the vinegar and sugar in a small saucepan and stir over low heat until the sugar dissolves. Remove from the heat and add the cucumber, chilli and extra spring (green) onion. Cool completely.

4 Preheat the oven to 220°C (425°F/Gas 7). Cut each pastry sheet into four squares. Drain the filling and divide into eight. Place one portion in the centre of each square and brush the edges with egg. Fold into a triangle and seal the edges with a fork.

5 Put the triangles on two lined baking trays (sheets), brush with egg and bake for 15 minutes. Serve with the dipping sauce.

BLOODY MARY OYSTER SHOTS

Preparation time:
10 minutes + 30 minutes refrigeration

Total cooking time:
Nil

Serves 12

INGREDIENTS

- ⅓ cup (80 ml/2¾ fl oz) vodka
- ½ cup (125 ml/4¼ fl oz) tomato juice
- 1 tablespoon lemon juice
- dash of Worcestershire sauce
- 2 drops of hot chilli (pepper) sauce
- pinch of celery salt
- 12 oysters
- 1 cucumber, peeled, seeded and finely julienned

1 Combine the vodka, tomato juice, lemon juice, Worcestershire sauce, hot chilli (pepper) sauce and celery salt, then refrigerate for 30 minutes, or until chilled. Just before serving, fill each shot glass about two-thirds full. Drop an oyster in each glass, then top with a teaspoon of cucumber. Crack some pepper over each shot glass, then serve.

NOTE: It is better to use oysters fresh from the shell rather than from a jar as they have a much better, fresher taste.

THINK AHEAD: The tomato mixture can be made a day ahead of time and kept in the fridge. Stir before serving.

VARIATION: If you think your guests are game enough for some fire in their evening, make chilled sake shots – fill each glass two-thirds full of sake, add an oyster, then garnish with cucumber.

SMOKED SALMON BREAD BASKETS

Preparation time:
20 minutes + cooling

Total cooking time:
10 minutes

Makes 24

INGREDIENTS

- 250 g (8¾ oz) smoked salmon
- 1 loaf white sliced bread
- ¼ cup (60 ml/2 fl oz) olive oil
- ⅓ cup (90 g/3¼ oz)
  whole-egg mayonnaise
- 2 teaspoons extra virgin olive oil
- 1 teaspoon white wine vinegar
- 1 teaspoon finely chopped fresh
  dill (dill weed)
- 3 teaspoons horseradish cream
- 3 tablespoons salmon roe

1 Preheat the oven to 180°C
(350°F/Gas 4). Cut the salmon
into strips. Flatten the bread to
2 mm (¹⁄₁₆ inch) with a rolling pin.
Cut out 24 rounds with a 7 cm
(2¾ inch) cutter. Brush both sides
of the rounds with olive oil and
push into the holes of two
12-hole flat-based patty (bun)
tins. Bake for 10 minutes, or
until crisp. Cool.

2 Stir the mayonnaise in a bowl
with the extra virgin olive oil,
vinegar, dill (dill weed) and
horseradish until combined.

3 Arrange folds of salmon in each
cooled bread case and top each
with 1 teaspoon of mayonnaise
mixture. Spoon ½ teaspoon
of salmon roe on top of each
before serving.

NOTE: The bread cases can be
made a day in advance and, when
completely cold, stored in an
airtight container. If they soften,
you can crisp them on a baking tray
(sheet) in a moderate oven for
5 minutes. Cool before filling.

ASPARAGUS AND PROSCIUTTO BUNDLES WITH HOLLANDAISE

Preparation time:
10 minutes

Total cooking time:
15 minutes

Makes 24

INGREDIENTS

- 24 spears fresh asparagus, trimmed
- 8 slices prosciutto, cut into thirds lengthways

HOLLANDAISE
- 175 g (6¼ oz) butter
- 4 egg yolks
- 1 tablespoon lemon juice
- ground white pepper

1 Blanch the asparagus in boiling salted water for 2 minutes, then drain and refresh in cold water. Pat dry, then cut the spears in half. Lay the bottom half of each spear next to its tip, then secure by wrapping a piece of prosciutto around the bundle.

2 To make the hollandaise, melt the butter in a small saucepan. Skim any froth off the top. Cool the butter a little. Combine the egg yolks and 2 tablespoons of water in a heatproof bowl placed over a saucepan of simmering water, making sure the base of the bowl does not touch the water. Using a wire whisk, beat for about 3 minutes, or until the mixture is thick and foamy. Make sure the bowl does not get too hot or you will end up with scrambled eggs. Add the butter slowly, a little at a time at first, whisking well between each addition. Keep adding the butter in a thin stream, whisking continuously, until all the butter has been used. Try to avoid using the milky whey in the bottom of the pan, but don't worry if a little gets in. Stir in the lemon juice and season with salt and white pepper. Place in a bowl and serve warm with the asparagus.

VOL-AU-VENTS

Preparation time:
20 minutes + 15 minutes refrigeration

Total cooking time:
30 minutes

Makes 4

INGREDIENTS

- 250 g (8¾ oz) puff pastry
- 1 egg, lightly beaten

SAUCE AND FILLING
- 40 g (1½ oz) butter
- 2 spring (green) onions, finely chopped
- 2 tablespoons plain (all-purpose) flour
- 1½ cups (375 ml/13 fl oz) milk
- your choice of filling (see NOTE)

1 Preheat the oven to 220°C (425°F/Gas 7). Line a baking tray (sheet) with baking paper. Roll out the pastry to a 20 cm (8 inch) square. Cut four circles of pastry with a 10 cm (4 inch) cutter. Place the rounds onto the tray (sheet) and score 6 cm (2½ inch) circles into the centre of the rounds with a cutter, taking care not to cut right through the pastry. Refrigerate for 15 minutes.

2 Using a floured knife blade, knock up the sides of each pastry round by indenting with a knife every 1 cm (½ inch) around the circumference. This will help the cases rise evenly. Carefully brush the pastry with the egg, avoiding the edge as any glaze spilt on the side will stop the pastry from rising.

3 Bake for 15–20 minutes, or until the pastry has risen and is golden brown and crisp. Cool on a wire rack. Remove the centre from each pastry circle and pull out and discard any partially cooked pastry from the centre. The pastry can be returned to the oven for 2 minutes to dry out if the centre is undercooked. The pastry cases are now ready to be filled with a hot filling before serving.

4 For the sauce, melt the butter in a saucepan, add the spring (green) onion and stir over low heat for 2 minutes, or until soft. Add the flour and stir for 2 minutes, or until lightly golden. Gradually add the milk, stirring until smooth. Stir constantly over medium heat for 4 minutes, or until the mixture boils and thickens. Season well. Remove and stir in your choice of filling before spooning into the cases to serve.

NOTE: Add 350 g (12¼ oz) of any of the following to your white sauce: sliced, cooked mushrooms; peeled, cooked prawns (shrimp); chopped, cooked chicken breast; poached, flaked salmon; dressed crab meat; oysters; steamed asparagus spears.

STORAGE: The cases can be made up to the 'knocking up' stage (see step 2) and then frozen.

THAI CHICKEN BALLS

Preparation time:
20 minutes

Total cooking time:
40 minutes

Serves 6

INGREDIENTS

- 1 kg (2 lb 3 oz) chicken mince (ground chicken)
- 1 cup (80 g/2¾ oz) fresh breadcrumbs
- 4 spring (green) onions, sliced
- 1 tablespoon ground coriander
- 1 cup (50 g/1¾ oz) chopped coriander (cilantro)
- ¼ cup (60 ml/2 fl oz) sweet chilli sauce (jalapeno jelly)
- 1–2 tablespoons lemon juice
- oil, for frying

1 Preheat the oven to moderately hot 200°C (400°F/Gas 6). Mix the mince (ground chicken) and breadcrumbs in a large bowl.

2 Add the spring (green) onion, ground and fresh coriander (cilantro), chilli sauce (jalapeno jelly) and lemon juice, and mix well. Using damp hands, form the mixture into evenly shaped balls that are either small enough to eat with your fingers or large enough to use as burgers.

3 Heat the oil in a deep frying pan, and shallow-fry the chicken balls in batches over high heat until browned all over. Place the chicken balls on a baking tray (sheet) and bake until cooked through. (The small chicken balls will take 5 minutes to cook and the larger ones will take 10–15 minutes.) This mixture also makes a delicious filling for sausage rolls.

ASPARAGUS AND ARTICHOKE QUICHES

Preparation time:
40 minutes + 30 minutes refrigeration

Total cooking time:
40 minutes

Makes 6

INGREDIENTS

- 1¼ cups (150 g/5¼ oz) plain (all-purpose) flour
- 90 g (3¼ oz) butter, chilled and cubed
- ½ cup (60 g/2 oz) grated Cheddar (American) cheese
- 2–3 tablespoons iced water

FILLING
- 1 bunch (155 g/5½ oz) asparagus, trimmed, cut into bite-size pieces
- 2 eggs
- ⅓ cup (80 ml/2¾ fl oz) cream
- ⅓ cup (40 g/1½ oz) grated Gruyère cheese
- 150 g (5¼ oz) marinated artichoke hearts, quartered

1 Process the flour and butter for about 15 seconds until crumbly. Add the cheese and water. Process in short bursts until the mixture comes together. Add a little more water if needed. Turn out onto a floured surface and gather into a ball. Wrap in plastic and refrigerate for 30 minutes.

2 Preheat the oven to 190°C (375°F/Gas 5). Grease six 8.5 cm (3¼ inch) loose-based fluted tart tins. Roll out the pastry to fit the tins, trimming off the excess. Prick the pastry bases with a fork, place on a baking tray (sheet) and bake for 10–12 minutes, or until the pastry is light and golden.

3 To make the filling, blanch the asparagus pieces in boiling salted water. Drain and refresh in iced water. Lightly beat the eggs, cream and half the cheese together and season with salt and black pepper.

4 Divide the artichokes and asparagus among the pastry shells, pour the egg and cream mixture over the top and sprinkle with the remaining cheese. Bake for 25 minutes, or until the filling is set and golden. If the pastry is overbrowning, cover with foil.

ROAST BEEF ON CROÛTES

Preparation time:
20 minutes + 3 hours
15 minutes standing
Total cooking time:
25 minutes
Makes 30

INGREDIENTS

- 300 g (10 oz) piece beef eye fillet (tenderloin)
- ⅓ cup (80 ml/2¾ fl oz) olive oil
- 2 cloves garlic, crushed
- 2 sprigs fresh thyme plus extra to garnish
- 10 slices white bread
- 1 large clove garlic, peeled, extra

HORSERADISH CREAM
- ⅓ cup (80 ml/2¾ fl oz) thick (double/heavy) cream
- 1 tablespoon horseradish (see NOTE)
- 1 teaspoon lemon juice

1 Place the beef in a non-metallic bowl, pour on the combined oil, garlic and thyme and toss to coat well. Cover with plastic wrap and marinate in the refrigerator for about 2–3 hours. Preheat the oven to moderately hot 200°C (400°F/Gas 6).

2 To make the croûtes, cut out three rounds from each slice of bread using a 5 cm (2 inch) fluted cutter. Place the rounds on a baking tray (sheet) and bake for 5 minutes each side, then rub the whole garlic clove over each side of the rounds and set aside.

3 To make the horseradish cream, put the cream in a small bowl and whisk lightly until thickened. Gently fold in the horseradish and lemon juice, then season with cracked black pepper. Refrigerate until ready to use.

4 Heat a roasting tin in the oven for 5 minutes. Remove the beef from the marinade, reserving the marinade. Generously season the beef on all sides with salt and pepper, then place it in the hot roasting tin and turn it so that all sides of the meat are sealed. Drizzle with 2 tablespoons of the reserved marinade, then roast for 10–12 minutes for rare, or until cooked to your liking. Remove from the oven, cover with foil and rest for 15 minutes before slicing thinly.

5 Arrange one slice of beef on each croûte (you may need to cut the slices in half if they are too big), and top with ½ teaspoon of the horseradish cream and a small sprig of fresh thyme. Serve immediately.

NOTE: Grated horseradish is readily available in small jars preserved in vinegar. Don't confuse it with horseradish sauce, which already has a cream base.

THINK AHEAD: The beef and croûtes can be prepared the day before serving. Leave the beef whole, covered, in the refrigerator and slice just before assembling. Store the croûtes in an airtight container lined with paper towels to absorb any excess oil.

VARIATION: For a spicy variation on this classic canapé, marinate the beef fillet in ⅓ cup (80 ml / 2¾ fl oz) olive oil, 2 cloves crushed garlic, 1 teaspoon paprika and ½ teaspoon cayenne (red) pepper. Top with a simple garlic cream, made by combining 1 clove crushed garlic with ½ cup (125 ml / 4¼ fl oz) lightly whipped thick (double / heavy) cream and some salt and cracked black pepper to taste.

MACADAMIA-CRUSTED CHICKEN STRIPS WITH MANGO SALSA

Preparation time:
25 minutes + 30 minutes refrigeration

Total cooking time:
15 minutes

Makes 24

INGREDIENTS

- 12 chicken tenderloins (700 g/
  1lb 9 oz), larger ones cut in half
- seasoned plain (all-purpose) flour,
  for dusting
- 2 eggs, lightly beaten
- 250 g (8¾ oz) macadamias,
  finely chopped
- 2 cups (160 g/5⅔ oz) fresh breadcrumbs
- oil, for deep-frying

MANGO SALSA
- 1 small mango, very finely diced
- 2 tablespoons finely diced red onion
- 2 tablespoons roughly chopped fresh
  coriander (cilantro) leaves
- 1 fresh green chilli, seeded and
  finely chopped
- 1 tablespoon lime juice

1 Cut the chicken into strips.
  Dust the chicken strips with the
  flour, then dip them in the egg
  and, finally, coat them in the
  combined nuts and breadcrumbs.
  Chill for at least 30 minutes to
  firm up.

2 To make the salsa, combine all
  the ingredients in a small bowl
  and season to taste with salt and
  black pepper.

3 Fill a large heavy-based saucepan
  or deep-fryer one-third full of
  oil and heat to 180°C (350°F),
  or until a cube of bread dropped
  in the oil browns in 15 seconds.
  Cook the chicken strips in
  batches for 2–3 minutes, or until
  golden brown all over, taking
  care not to burn the nuts. Drain
  on crumpled paper towels.
  Serve the chicken strips warm
  with the salsa.

THINK AHEAD: These are best
made on the day they are to be
served.

VARIATIONS: The chicken strips
are also very tasty served with
sweet chilli sauce (jalapeno jelly).
Try a different coating using
almonds or peanuts.

MEXICAN BITES

Preparation time:
40 minutes + 30 minutes refrigeration

Total cooking time:
5 minutes

Makes 36

INGREDIENTS

- 740 g (1 lb 10 oz) can red kidney beans, drained
- 1 teaspoon ground cumin
- 2 tablespoons olive oil
- ¼ teaspoon cayenne (red) pepper
- 1 avocado
- 1 small clove garlic, crushed
- 2 tablespoons sour cream
- 2 tablespoons lime juice
- 1 vine-ripened tomato, seeded and finely chopped
- 2 tablespoons finely chopped fresh coriander (cilantro)
- 250 g (8¾ oz) packet round white corn (tortilla) chips

1 To make the refried beans, put the red kidney beans in a bowl and mash with a potato masher, then add the cumin. Heat 1½ tablespoons of oil in a large non-stick frying pan and add the cayenne (red) pepper and mashed red kidney beans. Cook the mixture over medium–high heat for 2–3 minutes, stirring constantly. Allow to cool, then refrigerate for 30 minutes, or until cold.

2 Scoop the avocado flesh into a food processor and add the garlic, sour cream and 1 tablespoon of the lime juice. Process for a few minutes until it is a thick creamy paste, then add salt to taste. Refrigerate.

3 To make the salsa, mix together the tomato, coriander (cilantro) and the remaining oil and lime juice in a small bowl. Refrigerate until needed.

4 To assemble, lay out 36 round white corn (tortilla) chips. Put a heaped teaspoon of refried beans in the centre of each chip, add a teaspoon of the avocado cream and top each with half a teaspoon of the tomato salsa.

THINK AHEAD: The bean puree can be made 3 days in advance. Make the salsa up to 2 hours beforehand. Assemble just before serving.

ASPARAGUS AND MUSHROOM SALAD

Preparation time:
20 minutes

Total cooking time:
10 minutes

Serves 4

INGREDIENTS

- 155 g (5½ oz) asparagus spears
- 1 tablespoon wholegrain mustard
- ¼ cup (60 ml/2 fl oz) orange juice
- 2 tablespoons lemon juice
- 1 tablespoon lime juice
- 1 tablespoon orange zest
- 2 teaspoons lemon zest
- 2 teaspoons lime zest
- 2 cloves garlic, crushed
- ¼ cup (90 g/3¼ oz) honey
- 400 g (14 oz) button mushrooms, halved
- 150 g (5¼ oz) rocket (arugula)
- 1 red capsicum (pepper), cut into strips

1 Snap the woody ends from the asparagus spears and cut in half on the diagonal. Cook in boiling water for 1 minute, or until just tender. Drain, plunge into cold water and set aside.

2 Place the mustard, citrus juice and zest, garlic and honey in a large saucepan and season with black pepper. Bring to the boil, then reduce the heat and add the mushrooms, tossing for 2 minutes. Cool.

3 Remove the mushrooms from the sauce with a slotted spoon. Return the sauce to the heat, bring to the boil, then reduce the heat and simmer for 3–5 minutes, or until reduced and syrupy. Cool slightly.

4 Toss the mushrooms, rocket (arugula) leaves, capsicum (pepper) and asparagus. Put on a plate and drizzle with the sauce.

RED AND GREEN SALAD

Preparation time:
25 minutes

Total cooking time:
5 minutes

Serves 4–6

INGREDIENTS

- 200 g (7 oz) snow peas (mange tout), sliced diagonally
- 1 large red capsicum (pepper), sliced
- 4 leaves oak leaf lettuce
- 5 leaves green coral lettuce
- 250 g (8¾ oz) cherry tomatoes
- 60 g (2 oz) watercress sprigs
- Parmesan cheese, to serve

GARLIC CROUTONS
- 3 slices white bread
- ¼ cup (60 ml/2 fl oz) olive oil
- 1 clove garlic, crushed

DRESSING
- 2 tablespoons olive oil
- 1 tablespoon mayonnaise
- 1 tablespoon sour cream
- 2 tablespoons lemon juice
- 1 teaspoon soft brown sugar
- cracked black pepper

1 Wash the lettuce and tomatoes. Combine the snow peas (mange tout), red capsicum (pepper), watercress, lettuces and tomatoes in a large bowl.

2 To make Garlic Croutons: Remove the crusts from the bread slices. Cut the bread into 1 cm (½ inch) squares. Heat the olive oil in small, heavy-based pan and add the crushed garlic. Stir in the prepared bread cubes and cook until golden and crisp. Remove from the heat and leave to drain well on paper towels.

3 To make Dressing: Whisk all the
ingredients in a small bowl for
2 minutes or until combined.
Just before serving, pour the
dressing over the salad, stirring
until well combined. Top with the
Garlic Croutons and thin shavings
of Parmesan cheese.

CAESAR SALAD

Preparation time:
25 minutes

Total cooking time:
20 minutes

Serves 6

INGREDIENTS

- 1 small French bread stick
- 2 tablespoons olive oil
- 2 cloves garlic, halved
- 4 rashers bacon (trimmed of fat)
- 2 cos (romaine) lettuces
- 10 anchovy fillets, halved lengthways
- 1 cup (100 g/3½ oz) shaved Parmesan
- Parmesan shavings, extra, for serving

DRESSING
- 1 egg yolk
- 2 cloves garlic, crushed
- 2 teaspoons Dijon mustard
- 2 anchovy fillets
- 2 tablespoons white wine vinegar
- 1 tablespoon Worcestershire sauce
- ¾ cup (185 ml/6½ fl oz) olive oil

1 Preheat the oven to moderate 180°C (350°F/Gas 4). To make the croutons, cut the bread stick into 15 thin slices and brush both sides of each slice with oil. Spread them all on a baking tray (sheet) and bake for 10–15 minutes, or until golden brown. Leave to cool slightly, then rub each side of each slice with the cut edge of a garlic clove. The baked bread can then be broken roughly into pieces or cut into small cubes.

2 Cook the bacon under a hot grill (broiler) until crisp. Drain on paper towels until cooled, then break into chunky pieces.

3 Tear the lettuce into pieces and put in a large serving bowl with the bacon, anchovies, croutons and Parmesan.

4 For the dressing, place the egg yolks, garlic, mustard, anchovies, vinegar and Worcestershire sauce in a food processor or blender. Season and process for 20 seconds, or until smooth. With the motor running, add enough oil in a thin stream to make the dressing thick and creamy.

5 Drizzle the dressing over the salad and toss gently. Sprinkle the Parmesan shavings over the top and serve immediately.

HOT POTATO SALAD

Preparation time:
15 minutes

Total cooking time:
25 minutes

Serves 8

INGREDIENTS

- 4 rashers bacon
- 1.5 kg (3 lb 5 oz) small waxy red potatoes, unpeeled
- 4 spring (green) onions, sliced
- 3 tablespoons chopped fresh flat-leaf parsley

DRESSING
- ⅔ cup (170 ml / 5¾ fl oz) extra virgin olive oil
- 1 tablespoon Dijon mustard
- ⅓ cup (80 ml / 2¾ fl oz) white wine vinegar

1 Trim the rind and any excess fat from the bacon, then cook under a hot grill (broiler) until crisp. Chop into small pieces.

2 Steam or boil the potatoes for 10–15 minutes, or until just tender (pierce with the point of a small sharp knife – if the potato comes away easily it is ready). Don't let the skins break away. Drain and cool slightly.

3 For the dressing, whisk all the ingredients together in a jug.

4 Cut the potatoes into quarters and place in a bowl with half the bacon, the spring (green) onion, parsley and some salt and freshly ground black pepper. Pour in half the dressing and toss to coat the potatoes thoroughly. Transfer to a serving bowl, drizzle with the remaining dressing and sprinkle the remaining bacon over the top.

NOTE: The cooking time will depend on the size of the potatoes. The potatoes can be diced instead of quartered if you prefer.

RED-RICE SALAD

Preparation time:
20 minutes + cooling
Total cooking time:
50 minutes
Serves 4

INGREDIENTS

- 1 cup (220 g/7¾ oz) Camargue red rice
- 1 red capsicum (pepper)
- 1 yellow capsicum (pepper)
- ⅓ cup (80 ml/2¾ fl oz) olive oil
- 1 red onion, cut into slivers
- 2 zucchini (courgettes), diced
- 1 tablespoon butter
- 1 garlic clove, crushed
- 1 chicken breast with skin on
- 2 tablespoons lemon juice
- 2 tablespoons chopped basil
- 2 tablespoons chopped parsley

1 Put the rice in a saucepan with plenty of boiling water and cook for 30 minutes, or until tender. Drain well, then cool.

2 Cut the red and yellow capsicums (peppers) in half lengthways. Remove the seeds and membrane, then cut the flesh into large, flattish pieces. Grill (broil) or hold over a gas flame until the skin blackens and blisters. Place on a cutting board, cover with a tea towel and allow to cool. Peel the skin off and cut the flesh into smaller pieces. Add the capsicum (pepper) strips to the rice.

3 Heat the oil in a frying pan, then cook the onion and zucchini (courgette) until lightly charred around the edges. Add the onion and zucchini (courgette) to the rice.

4 Mix the butter with the garlic. Push the mixture under the skin of the chicken breast so it is evenly distributed. Grill (broil) the chicken on both sides until the skin is crisp and the breast is cooked through. Leave the chicken to rest for 2 minutes, then slice it into strips. (You can discard the skin, if you like.)

5 Add the chicken slices to the rice with any juices. Add the lemon juice, any remaining olive oil and the herbs, and toss together. Season well and serve immediately.

COOKED VEGETABLE SALAD

Preparation time:
45 minutes + 20
minutes standing

Total cooking time:
15 minutes

Serves 4

INGREDIENTS

- 1 small turnip, peeled, cut into
  fine strips
- 2 teaspoons salt
- ½ cup (80 g/2¾ oz) pine nuts
- 2 tablespoons sesame oil
- 1 tablespoon oil
- 2 cloves garlic, finely chopped
- 1 large onion, thinly sliced into rings
- 2 sticks (ribs) celery, sliced
- 200 g (7 oz) button mushrooms, sliced
- 1 large carrot, cut into fine strips

- ½ red capsicum (pepper), cut into
  fine strips
- 4 spring (green) onions, chopped

DRESSING
- ¼ cup (60 ml/2 fl oz) soy sauce
- 1 tablespoon white vinegar
- 3 cm (1¼ inch) piece fresh ginger
  (gingerroot), very finely sliced and
  cut into fine strips
- 1–2 teaspoons soft brown sugar

1 Place the turnip on a plate lined
  with a paper towel. Sprinkle
  with salt, and set aside for at least
  20 minutes. Rinse the turnip
  under cold water and pat dry
  with paper towels.

2 Toast the pine nuts in a dry pan
  over medium heat for 3 to 4
  minutes, shaking the pan gently,
  until the seeds are golden brown;
  remove from the pan at once to
  prevent burning and set aside.

3 Heat the combined oils in a large frying pan or wok. Stir-fry (scramble-fry) the turnip, garlic and onion for 3 minutes over medium heat until lightly golden. Add the celery, mushrooms, carrot, red capsicum (pepper) and spring (green) onion and toss well; cover and steam for 1 minute. Remove the vegetables from the wok and cool.

4 To make Dressing: Combine the soy sauce, vinegar, ginger (gingerroot) and sugar in a bowl.

5 Pour the dressing over the cooled vegetables and toss. Arrange them on a serving plate and sprinkle over the pine nuts. Serve with steamed rice, if you like.

CHEF'S SALAD

Preparation time:
25 minutes

Total cooking time:
Nil

Serves 4

INGREDIENTS

DRESSING
- ½ cup (125 ml/4¼ fl oz) extra virgin olive oil
- 2 tablespoons white wine vinegar
- 1 teaspoon sugar

- 1 iceberg lettuce
- 2 tomatoes, cut into wedges
- 2 celery sticks (ribs), cut into julienne strips
- 1 cooked chicken breast fillet, cut into thin strips
- 200 g (7 oz) ham, cut into thin strips
- 60 g (2 oz) Swiss cheese, cut into strips
- 3 hard-boiled eggs, cut into wedges
- 6 radishes, sliced

1 Whisk the dressing ingredients together in a small jug until well combined. Season, to taste, with salt and freshly ground black pepper.

2 Coarsely shred the lettuce leaves and divide among serving plates. Top with layers of the tomato, celery, chicken, ham, cheese, egg and radish. Drizzle the dressing over the salad and serve immediately.

GREEN TEA NOODLE SALAD WITH LAMB AND TOMATO

Preparation time:
20 minutes + 2 hours
marinating

Total cooking time:
20 minutes

Serves 4

INGREDIENTS

- 1 teaspoon hot mustard
- 2 tablespoons vegetable oil
- ¼ cup (60 ml/2 fl oz) balsamic vinegar
- 400 g (14 oz) lamb loin fillets, thinly sliced across the grain
- 250 g (8¾ oz) chasoba noodles (see NOTE)
- ¼ cup (60 ml/2 fl oz) light soy sauce
- 2 tablespoons mirin
- 1–2 teaspoons sesame oil
- ½ teaspoon sugar

- 2 Lebanese cucumbers, cut in half lengthways and thinly sliced on the diagonal
- 2 large tomatoes, cut into 1 cm (½ inch) cubes
- ½ cup (15 g/½ oz) fresh coriander (cilantro) leaves
- 2 spring (green) onions, thinly sliced on the diagonal
- 1 tablespoon sesame seeds, lightly toasted

1 Combine the mustard, 1 tablespoon of the oil, 1 tablespoon of the vinegar and ½ teaspoon pepper in a large non-metallic bowl. Add the lamb and toss. Cover, then refrigerate for 2 hours.

2 Add the noodles to a large saucepan of boiling water and stir to separate. Return to the boil, adding 1 cup (250 ml/8½ fl oz) cold water and repeat this step three times, as it comes to the boil. Drain and rinse under cold water. Place in a large bowl.

3 Combine the soy sauce, mirin, sesame oil, sugar, the remaining balsamic vinegar and ½ teaspoon salt and stir until the sugar dissolves. Toss half of the dressing through the noodles.

4 Place the cucumber, tomato and ½ teaspoon salt in a bowl and toss well. Add to the noodles with the coriander (cilantro) and spring (green) onion and toss well.

5 Heat a wok over high heat, add the remaining oil and swirl to coat. Drain the lamb, then, using tongs or a slotted spoon, add the lamb to the wok in two batches, and stir-fry (scramble-fry) each batch for 2–3 minutes, or until the lamb is seared and cooked to your liking. Divide the noodle salad among serving plates, then top with the lamb. Drizzle with as much of the dressing as you like. Sprinkle with the sesame seeds and serve.

NOTE: Chasoba noodles are soba noodles that have had green tea powder added to them.

SALAD NICOISE

Preparation time:
30 minutes

Total cooking time:
15 minutes

Serves 4

INGREDIENTS

- 3 eggs
- 2 vine-ripened tomatoes
- 175 g (6¼ oz) baby green beans, trimmed
- ½ cup (125 ml/4¼ fl oz) olive oil
- 2 tablespoons white wine vinegar
- 1 large clove garlic, halved
- 325 g (11½ oz) iceberg lettuce heart, cut into 8 wedges
- 1 small red capsicum (pepper), seeded and sliced thinly
- 1 Lebanese cucumber, cut into thin 5 cm (2 inch) lengths

- 1 stick (rib) celery, cut into thin 5 cm (2 inch) lengths
- ¼ large red onion, thinly sliced
- 2 × 185 g (6½ oz) cans tuna, drained, broken into chunks
- 12 Kalamata olives
- 45 g (1⅔ oz) can anchovy fillets, drained
- 2 teaspoons baby capers
- 12 small fresh basil leaves

1 Place the eggs in a saucepan of cold water. Bring to the boil, then reduce the heat and simmer for 10 minutes. Stir during the first few minutes to centre the yolks. Cool under cold water, then peel and cut into quarters. Meanwhile, score a cross in the base of each tomato and place in a bowl of boiling water for 10 seconds. Plunge into cold water and peel away from the cross. Cut each tomato into eight.

2 Cook the beans in a saucepan of boiling water for 2 minutes, rinse under cold water, then drain.

3 For the dressing, place the oil and vinegar in a jar and shake to combine.

4 Rub the garlic over the base and sides of a platter. Arrange the lettuce over the base. Layer the egg, tomato, beans, red capsicum (pepper), cucumber and celery over the lettuce. Scatter the onion and tuna over them, then the olives, anchovies, capers and basil. Drizzle with dressing and serve.

WILD RICE SALAD WITH CHINESE ROAST DUCK

Preparation time:
15 minutes

Total cooking time:
50 minutes

Serves 4–6

INGREDIENTS

- 1 cup (200 g/7 oz) wild rice
- 1 cup (200 g/7 oz) basmati or jasmine rice
- 16 thin asparagus spears, sliced
- 8 spring (green) onions, thinly sliced
- 100 g (3½ oz) pecans, roughly chopped
- 100 g (3½ oz) dried cranberries
- zest and juice 1 orange
- 1 whole Chinese roast duck

DRESSING
- ½ cup (125 ml/4¼ fl oz) soy sauce
- 2 tablespoons sugar
- 1½ tablespoons balsamic vinegar
- 1½ tablespoons peanut oil
- 2 teaspoons sesame oil
- 2 teaspoons grated ginger (gingerroot)
- 2 small red chillies, finely chopped

1 Put the wild rice in a saucepan of cold, salted water, bring to the boil and cook for 30 minutes. Add the basmati or jasmine rice and continue to cook for a further 10 minutes, or until both rices are just cooked. Drain and refresh under cold water, then drain again and transfer to a large bowl.

2 Blanch the asparagus in a saucepan of boiling water, then drain and refresh under cold water. Add to the bowl with the rice.

3 Add the spring (green) onions, pecans, dried cranberries and orange zest to the rice and mix together well.

4 Combine all the dressing
   ingredients and the orange juice
   in a screw-top jar and shake well.

5 Heat the oven to 200°C (400°F/
   Gas 6). Remove the skin from
   the duck and break it into rough
   pieces. Shred the duck meat and
   add it to the salad. Place the skin

on a baking tray (sheet) and bake
for 5 minutes, or until crispy.
Drain on paper towel, then slice.

6 Pour the dressing over the salad.
   Toss everything together. Serve
   the salad in bowls, topped with
   pieces of crispy duck skin.

THAI PORK NOODLE SALAD

Preparation time:
20 minutes

Total cooking time:
35 minutes

Serves 4–6

INGREDIENTS

BROTH
- 1 cup (250 ml/8½ fl oz) chicken stock (broth)
- 3 coriander (cilantro) roots
- 2 fresh kaffir lime leaves
- 3 × 3 cm (1¼ × 1¼ inch) piece fresh ginger (gingerroot), sliced

- 30 g (1 oz) fresh black fungus
- 100 g (3½ oz) cellophane noodles or dried rice vermicelli
- 1 small fresh red chilli, seeded and thinly sliced
- 2 red Asian shallots, thinly sliced
- 2 spring (green) onions, thinly sliced
- 2 cloves garlic, crushed
- 1 tablespoon vegetable oil

- 250 g (8¾ oz) pork mince (ground pork)
- 2½ tablespoons lime juice
- 2½ tablespoons fish sauce
- 1½ tablespoons grated palm sugar
- ¼ teaspoon ground white pepper
- ½ cup (15 g/½ oz) fresh coriander (cilantro) leaves, chopped
- oak leaf or coral lettuce, torn or shredded
- lime wedges, to garnish
- fresh red chilli, extra, cut into strips, to garnish
- fresh coriander (cilantro) leaves, extra, to garnish (optional)

1 To make the broth, put the chicken stock (broth), coriander (cilantro) roots, lime leaves, ginger (gingerroot) and 1 cup (250 ml/8½ fl oz) water in a wok. Simmer for 25 minutes, or until it has reduced to ¾ cup (185 ml/6½ fl oz). Strain.

2 Discard the woody stems from the fungus, then thinly slice. Soak the noodles in boiling water for 3–4 minutes, or until pliable. Rinse, drain, then cut into 3 cm (1¼ inch) lengths. Combine the noodles, fungus, chilli, shallots, spring (green) onion and garlic.

3 Heat a clean, dry wok over high heat, add the oil and swirl to coat. Add the pork mince (ground pork) and stir-fry (scramble-fry), breaking up any lumps, for 1–2 minutes, or until the pork changes colour and is cooked. Add the broth and bring the mixture to the boil over high

heat. Boil for 1 minute, then drain, and add the pork to the noodle mixture.

4 Combine the lime juice, fish sauce, palm sugar and white pepper, stirring until the sugar is dissolved. Add to the pork mixture with the coriander (cilantro) and mix well. Season to taste with salt.

5 Arrange the lettuce on a serving dish, spoon on the pork and noodle mixture and garnish with the lime, chilli and, if desired, fresh coriander (cilantro) leaves.

CHICKEN AND VEGETABLE SALAD

Preparation time:
30 minutes

Total cooking time:
20 minutes

Serves 4–6

INGREDIENTS

- 400 g (14 oz) chicken breast fillets
- 1 cup (250 ml/8½ fl oz) water
- 3 slices fresh ginger (gingerroot)
- 2 stems lemongrass (white part only), roughly chopped
- 2 tablespoons fish sauce
- 250 g (8¾ oz) broccoli, cut into florets
- 150 g (5¼ oz) fresh baby corn
- 100 g (3½ oz) snow peas (mange tout), trimmed
- 1 red capsicum (pepper), cut into strips

- 3 spring (green) onions, cut into strips
- ½ cup (125 ml/4¼ fl oz) sweet chilli sauce (jalapeno jelly)
- 2 tablespoons honey or 2 tablespoons grated palm sugar mixed with a little warm water
- 2 tablespoons lime juice
- 2 teaspoons grated lime rind
- ¼ cup (7 g/¼ oz) fresh coriander (cilantro) leaves

1 Slice the chicken into short, thin strips.

2 Place the water, ginger (gingerroot), lemongrass and fish sauce in a frying pan. Bring the mixture to the boil, reduce the heat slightly and simmer for 5 minutes.

3 Add the chicken to the pan and cook in the hot liquid for 5 minutes, stirring occasionally. Drain and allow to cool. Discard liquid.

4 Bring a large pan of water to the boil and cook the broccoli, corn, snow peas (mange tout), red capsicum (pepper) and spring (green) onion for 2 minutes. Drain and plunge into iced water; drain again.

5 Combine the sweet chilli sauce (jalapeno jelly), honey, lime juice and rind in a small bowl and mix well. Arrange the vegetables and chicken on a serving platter. Pour the sauce over the top and toss gently. Sprinkle over the coriander (cilantro) leaves.

SPICY CABBAGE ROLLS

Preparation time:
40 minutes

Total cooking time:
30 minutes

Serves 6

INGREDIENTS

- 6 large green cabbage leaves

FILLING
- 2 teaspoons olive oil
- 4 spring (green) onions, finely chopped
- 1 clove garlic, crushed
- 2 tablespoons tomato paste (tomato puree)
- ½ cup (75 g/2⅔ oz) dried currants
- 2 tablespoons slivered almonds
- 1 teaspoon cumin seeds

- ½ teaspoon ground cinnamon
- 2 tablespoons finely chopped fresh parsley
- 2½ cups (470 g/1 lb ½ oz) cooked long-grain rice
- 1 cup (250 ml/8½ fl oz) vegetable stock (broth)

YOGHURT SAUCE
- ¾ cup (185 g/6½ oz) plain yoghurt
- 1 teaspoon ground cumin
- 1 tablespoon finely chopped fresh mint

1 Preheat the oven to moderately hot 190°C (375°F/Gas 5). Brush a deep ovenproof dish with melted butter or oil.

2 Blanch the cabbage leaves in boiling water for 10 seconds or until they are soft and pliable. Drain; remove and discard the hard stalk from the leaves. Set leaves aside.

3 To make Filling: Heat the oil in a large pan. Add the spring (green) onions and garlic and cook over medium heat for 30 seconds. Add the tomato paste (tomato puree), dried currants, almonds, cumin seeds, cinnamon, parsley and rice; stir until well combined. Remove from heat and cool slightly.

4 Place 3 tablespoons of filling on the edge of one cabbage leaf. Roll into a neat parcel, folding in the edges while rolling. Repeat with the remaining filling and leaves. Place the cabbage parcels, flap-side down, in prepared dish and pour the stock (broth) over them. Invert an ovenproof plate on top of the cabbage parcels to prevent them from falling apart. Cover with a lid or foil; bake for 20–25 minutes or until heated through.

5 To make Yoghurt Sauce: Mix together the yoghurt, cumin and mint in a bowl. Serve the cabbage rolls warm or cold with Yoghurt Sauce.

NOTE: Make the Yoghurt Sauce just before serving. If the leaves are difficult to remove from cabbage, boil the whole cabbage in enough water to cover, for about 3–4 minutes. Remove and cool slightly. The leaves should separate easily.

CARPACCIO

Preparation time:
15 minutes + freezing

Total cooking time:
Nil

Serves 8

INGREDIENTS

- 400 g (14 oz) beef eye fillet (tenderloin)
- 1 tablespoon extra virgin olive oil
- rocket (arugula) leaves, torn
- 60 g (2 oz) Parmesan, shaved
- black (ripe) olives, cut into slivers

1 Remove all the visible fat and sinew from the beef, then freeze for 1–2 hours, until firm but not solid. This makes the meat easier to slice thinly.

2 Cut paper-thin slices of beef with a large, sharp knife. Arrange on a serving platter and allow to return to room temperature.

3 Just before serving, drizzle with oil, then scatter with rocket (arugula), Parmesan and olives.

IN ADVANCE: The beef can be cut into slices a few hours in advance, covered and refrigerated. Drizzle with oil and garnish with the other ingredients just before serving.

CHICKEN AND CORN PIES

Preparation time:
25 minutes + 2 hours refrigeration

Total cooking time:
50 minutes

Makes 6

INGREDIENTS

- 1 tablespoon olive oil
- 650 g (1 lb 7 oz) chicken thigh fillets, cut into small pieces
- 1 tablespoon grated fresh ginger (gingerroot)
- 400 g (14 oz) oyster mushrooms, halved
- 3 corn cobs, kernels removed
- ½ cup (125 ml/4¼ fl oz) chicken stock (broth)
- 2 tablespoons kecap manis (Indonesian soy sauce)
- 2 tablespoons cornflour (cornstarch)
- 90 g (3¼ oz) coriander (cilantro) leaves, chopped
- 6 sheets shortcrust (pie) pastry
- milk, to glaze

1 Grease six 10 cm (4 inch) metal pie tins. Heat the oil in a large frying pan over high heat and add the chicken. Cook for 5 minutes, or until golden. Add the ginger (gingerroot), mushrooms and corn and cook for 5–6 minutes, or until the chicken is just cooked through. Add the stock (broth) and kecap manis (Indonesian soy sauce). Mix the cornflour (cornstarch) with 2 tablespoons water, then stir into the pan. Boil for 2 minutes before adding the coriander (cilantro). Cool then chill for 2 hours.

2 Preheat the oven to 180°C (350°F/Gas 4). Using a saucer as a guide, cut a 15 cm (6 inch) round from each sheet of shortcrust (pie) pastry and line the pie tins. Fill the shells with the cooled filling, then cut out another six rounds large enough to make the lids. Trim away any extra pastry and seal the edges with a fork. Decorate with pastry scraps. Prick a few holes in the top of each pie, brush with a little milk and bake for 35 minutes until golden.

GOLDEN SLICES IN BLACK BEAN SAUCE

Preparation time:
20 minutes

Total cooking time:
35 minutes

Serves 4

INGREDIENTS

- 500 g (1 lb 2 oz) medium eggplant (aubergine)
- ⅓ cup (80 ml/2¾ fl oz) oil
- 4 cloves garlic, finely chopped
- 4 cm (1½ inch) piece fresh ginger (gingerroot), grated
- 2 medium onions, finely chopped
- ⅓ cup (80 ml/2¾ fl oz) chicken stock (broth)
- 2 teaspoons canned black beans, rinsed well, roughly chopped
- 2 tablespoons oyster sauce
- 1 tablespoon soy sauce
- 2 teaspoons fish sauce
- 4 spring (green) onions, sliced into long diagonal strips

1 Slice the eggplant (aubergine) into long slices and lightly brush each side with oil.

2 Heat a frying pan over moderately low heat; add the eggplant (aubergine), 4 to 5 slices at a time, and cook until golden on both sides; remove from the pan. Do not hurry this process as cooking the eggplant (aubergine) slowly allows the natural sugars to caramelise and produces a wonderful flavour. If the eggplant (aubergine) begins to burn, reduce the heat and sprinkle it with a little water.

3 Increase the heat to moderately high and add any remaining oil, the garlic, ginger (gingerroot), onion and about 1 tablespoon of the chicken stock (broth); cover and cook for 3 minutes. Add the remaining stock (broth), black beans, oyster sauce, soy sauce and fish sauce. Bring to the boil and cook for 2 minutes. Return the eggplant (aubergine) to the pan and simmer for 2 minutes or until it is heated through. Scatter over the spring (green) onion and serve.

NOTE: Always rinse black beans very well before using, as they are extremely salty. They will keep indefinitely if refrigerated after opening.

SCALLOPS ON ASIAN RISOTTO CAKES

Preparation time:
35 minutes + 3 hours
10 minutes refrigeration

Total cooking time:
40 minutes

Serves 4

INGREDIENTS

- 2 cups (500 ml/17 fl oz) vegetable stock (broth)
- 2 tablespoons mirin
- 1 stem lemongrass (white part only), bruised
- 2 kaffir (makrut) lime leaves
- 3 coriander (cilantro) roots
- 2 tablespoons fish sauce
- 20 g (⅔ oz) butter
- 2–3 tablespoons peanut oil
- 3 red Asian shallots, thinly sliced
- 4 spring (green) onions, chopped
- 3 garlic cloves, chopped
- 2 tablespoons finely chopped ginger (gingerroot)
- 1¼ teaspoons white pepper

- ⅔ cup (140 g/5 oz) arborio rice
- 2 tablespoons toasted unsalted chopped peanuts
- 1 cup (50 g/1¾ oz) chopped coriander (cilantro) leaves
- 2 garlic cloves, chopped, extra
- 1 teaspoon finely chopped ginger (gingerroot), extra
- ¼ cup (60 ml/2 fl oz) lime juice
- 1–2 teaspoons grated palm sugar
- vegetable oil, for pan-frying
- plain (all-purpose) flour, to dust
- 1 tablespoon vegetable oil, extra
- 16 large white scallops without roe, beard removed
- lime wedges, to serve

1 Heat the stock (broth), mirin, lemongrass, lime leaves, coriander (cilantro) roots, half the fish sauce and 1 cup (250 ml/8½ fl oz) water in a saucepan, bring to the boil, then reduce the heat and keep at a simmer.

2 Heat the butter and 1 tablespoon of the peanut oil in a large saucepan over medium heat until bubbling. Add the shallots, spring (green) onion, garlic, ginger (gingerroot) and 1 teaspoon of the white pepper and cook for 2–3 minutes, or until fragrant and the onion is soft. Add the rice and stir until coated.

3 Add ½ cup (125 ml / 4¼ fl oz) of the stock (broth) (avoid the lemongrass and coriander (cilantro) roots). Stir constantly over medium heat until nearly all the liquid is absorbed. Continue adding the stock (broth) ½ cup (125 ml / 4¼ fl oz) at a time, stirring constantly, for 20–25 minutes, or until all the stock (broth) is absorbed and the rice is tender and creamy. Remove from the heat, cool, then cover and refrigerate for 3 hours, or until cold.

4 To make the pesto, combine the peanuts, coriander (cilantro), extra garlic and ginger (gingerroot) and the remaining pepper in a blender or food processor and process until finely chopped. With the motor running, slowly add the lime juice, sugar and remaining fish sauce and peanut oil and process until smooth – you might not need all the oil.

5 Divide the risotto into four balls, then mould into patties. Cover and refrigerate for 10 minutes. Heat the oil in a large frying pan over medium heat. Dust the patties with flour and cook in batches for 2 minutes each side, or until crisp. Drain on paper towels. Cover and keep warm.

6 Heat the extra oil in a clean frying pan over high heat. Cook the scallops in batches for 1 minute each side. Serve a patty with four scallops, some pesto and lime wedges.

PORK AND LETTUCE PARCELS

Preparation time:
1 hour

Total cooking time:
55 minutes

Serves 4–6

INGREDIENTS

- 500 g (1 lb 2 oz) pork loin
- 5 cm (2 inch) piece fresh ginger (gingerroot), thinly sliced
- 1 tablespoon fish sauce
- 20 spring (green) onions (choose thin ones)
- 2 soft-leaf lettuces
- 1 Lebanese cucumber, thinly sliced
- 3 tablespoons fresh mint
- 3 tablespoons fresh coriander (cilantro) leaves
- 2 green chillies, seeded and very finely sliced, optional
- 2 teaspoons sugar
- A dipping sauce, such as lemon and garlic, to serve

1 Place the pork, ginger (gingerroot) and fish sauce in a large pan and cover with cold water. Bring to the boil, reduce the heat and simmer, covered, for about 45 minutes or until the pork is tender. Remove the pork and allow to cool; discard the liquid.

2 Trim both ends from all the spring (green) onions so that you have long stems of equal length. Bring a large pot of water to the boil and blanch the spring (green) onions 2 to 3 at a time for about 2 minutes, or until softened. Remove the spring (green) onions from the hot water with tongs and place them in a bowl of iced water. Drain them and lay them flat and straight on a tray to be used later.

3 Separate the lettuce into leaves. If the leaves have a firm section at the base, trim this away (or making a neat parcel will be difficult).

4 When the pork is cool enough to handle, cut it into thin slices and finely shred each slice. Spread out a lettuce leaf, place about 1 tablespoon of the shredded pork in the centre of the leaf. Top with a few slices of cucumber, a few mint and coriander (cilantro) leaves, a little chilli, if using, and a light sprinkling of sugar. Fold a section of the lettuce over the filling, bring in the sides to meet each other and carefully roll up the parcel. Tie one of the spring (green) onions around the parcel; trim off the excess or tie it into a bow. Repeat with the remaining ingredients. Arrange the parcels on a serving platter and serve with a dipping sauce.

SMOKED SALMON IN DILL DRESSING

Preparation time:
15 minutes

Total cooking time:
Nil

Serves 4

INGREDIENTS

- 400 g (14 oz) smoked salmon
- 2 tablespoons light olive oil
- 2 tablespoons oil
- 2 tablespoons lemon juice
- 3 teaspoons soft brown sugar
- 3 tablespoons chopped fresh dill (dill weed)

1 Arrange the smoked salmon slices in a single layer, on individual plates or a large platter.

2 Combine the oils, juice and sugar in a bowl and stir until the sugar dissolves. Season, to taste, then mix in 2 tablespoons of the dill (dill weed).

3 Drizzle the dressing over the salmon. Using the back of a spoon, cover the salmon with the dressing. Sprinkle with the remaining dill (dill weed) and some cracked black pepper and serve with extra lemon wedges and slices of rye bread.

BARBECUED QUAIL

Preparation time:
30 minutes + at least 3 hours chilling

Total cooking time:
10 minutes

Serves 6

INGREDIENTS

- 6 quails
- 1 cup (250 ml/8½ fl oz) dry red wine
- 2 sticks (ribs) celery, including tops, chopped
- 1 carrot, chopped
- 1 small onion, chopped
- 1 bay leaf, torn into small pieces
- 1 teaspoon allspice
- 1 teaspoon dried thyme
- 2 cloves garlic, crushed
- 2 tablespoons olive oil
- 2 tablespoons lemon juice
- 1 lemon, cut into wedges, for serving

1 To prepare the quails, use poultry shears to cut down either side of the backbone on each quail, then discard the backbone. Remove the innards, wash the insides of the quails and pat dry with paper towels. Place the quails breast-side-up on the bench, open them out flat and gently press to flatten. With the poultry shears, cut each quail in half through the breast, then cut each quail half in half again, into the thigh and drumstick piece and breast and wing piece.

2 In a non-metallic bowl, combine the wine, celery, carrot, onion, bay leaf and allspice. Add the quail and stir to coat. Cover and marinate in the refrigerator for 3 hours, or preferably overnight, stirring occasionally. Drain and sprinkle with thyme and some salt and pepper.

3 Whisk the garlic, oil and lemon juice together in a small bowl.

4 Heat a lightly oiled barbecue plate until hot or heat a grill (broiler) to its highest setting. Reduce the heat to medium and cook the quail breast pieces for 4–5 minutes on each side and the drumstick pieces for 3 minutes on each side, or until tender and cooked through. Brush frequently with the lemon mixture during cooking. Serve hot, with lemon wedges.

RICE ROUNDS WITH DIPPING SAUCE

Preparation time:
30 minutes

Total cooking time:
15 minutes

Makes 6

INGREDIENTS

DIPPING SAUCE
- ½ cup (125 ml/4¼ fl oz) rice vinegar
- ½ cup (110 g/3¾ oz) sugar
- 2 garlic cloves, crushed
- 2 bird's eye chillies, finely chopped

- 2 eggs
- 1 tablespoon fish sauce
- ½ teaspoon sugar
- 3 cups (650 g/1 lb 7 oz) cooked glutinous short-grain rice, well drained

1 Preheat the grill (broiler) to its highest setting. To make the dipping sauce, combine all the ingredients in a small bowl and stir until the sugar is dissolved.

2 Beat the eggs with the fish sauce, sugar and a pinch of black pepper.

3 Divide the cooked rice into six portions and form each one into three small balls. Press each ball to flatten. Thread three flat rounds onto each skewer.

4 Line a grill tray (broiler sheet) with foil and brush it lightly with oil. Dip each rice skewer into the egg mixture, shake off any excess and put it on the grill tray (broiler sheet). Grill (broil) the rice until it is browned on one side, then turn it over and cook the other side. Serve with the dipping sauce.

SALMON SATAY WITH GINGER LIME MAYONNAISE

Preparation time:
30 minutes + chilling

Total cooking time:
4 minutes

Makes 24 skewers

INGREDIENTS

- 500 g (1 lb 2 oz) Atlantic salmon (or ocean trout) fillet
- 24 small wooden skewers
- light olive oil

GINGER LIME MAYONNAISE
- 1 cup (250 g/8¾ oz) whole egg mayonnaise
- ¼ cup (60 g/2 oz) natural yoghurt
- 1 teaspoon finely grated fresh ginger (gingerroot)
- 1 teaspoon finely grated lime rind
- 2 teaspoons lime juice

1 Remove the skin from the salmon. Use kitchen tweezers to remove any bones from the fish, then wrap the fish in plastic wrap and freeze for 1 hour. Soak small wooden satay sticks in cold water for 30 minutes (this will prevent them burning during cooking).

2 Cut the salmon fillets into 5 cm (2 inch) strips. Thread the strips loosely onto the satay sticks and place them on an oiled tray (sheet). Brush all over with oil and season, to taste, with salt and freshly ground pepper. Grill (broil) in two batches for 2 minutes, taking care not to overcook. Serve with the ginger lime mayonnaise.

3 To make ginger lime mayonnaise, place the mayonnaise in a small bowl and stir until smooth. Add the yoghurt, ginger (gingerroot) and lime rind and juice. Add salt and pepper, to taste, and stir until blended thoroughly. Chill for at least 1 hour.

IN ADVANCE: The skewers can be
assembled up to 1 hour in advance
and refrigerated. Cook just prior to
serving. Make the mayonnaise up to

2 days ahead and store, covered,
in the refrigerator. The prepared
skewers can be frozen in a single
layer for up to 2 months.

SWEET BRAISED PUMPKIN

Preparation time:
20 minutes

Total cooking time:
15 minutes

Serves 4

INGREDIENTS

- 750 g (1 lb 10 oz) pumpkin
- 1½ tablespoons oil
- 3 cloves garlic, finely chopped
- 4 cm (1½ inch) piece fresh ginger (gingerroot), grated
- 6 red Asian shallots, chopped
- 1 tablespoon soft brown sugar
- ½ cup (125 ml/4¼ fl oz) chicken stock (broth)
- 2 tablespoons fish sauce
- 1 tablespoon lime juice

1 Peel the pumpkin and cut it into large chunks.

2 Heat the oil in a heavy-based frying pan; add the garlic, ginger (gingerroot) and shallots and cook over medium heat for 3 minutes, stirring regularly.

3 Add the pumpkin and sprinkle with the sugar. Cook for 7 to 8 minutes, turning the pieces regularly, until the pumpkin is golden and just tender.

4 Add the chicken stock (broth) and fish sauce, bring to the boil, then reduce the heat and simmer until all the liquid has evaporated, turning the pumpkin over regularly. Sprinkle with the lime juice, season to taste with salt and pepper, and serve. Delicious as an accompaniment to meat dishes such as curries, or on its own with plenty of steamed rice.

NOTE: The sweeter pumpkins, such as butternut pumpkin (squash) and Japanese pumpkin, will produce a dish with a delicious flavour and soft texture.

FRENCH ONION SOUP

Preparation time:
30 minutes

Total cooking time:
1 hour 30 minutes

Serves 4

INGREDIENTS

- 50 g (1¾ oz) butter
- 1 tablespoon olive oil
- 1 kg (2 lb 3 oz) onions, thinly sliced into rings
- 3 × 420 g (14¾ oz) cans chicken or beef consommé
- ½ cup (125 ml/4¼ fl oz) dry sherry
- ½ French bread stick
- ⅓ cup (35 g/1¼ oz) grated Parmesan
- 1 cup (125 g/4⅓ oz) finely grated Cheddar (American) cheese or Gruyère
- 1 tablespoon finely chopped fresh parsley, to serve

1 Heat the butter and oil in a large saucepan, then add the onion and cook, stirring frequently, over low heat for 45 minutes, or until softened and translucent. Do not rush this stage – cook the onion thoroughly so that it caramelises and the flavours develop.

2 Add the consommé, sherry and 1 cup (250 ml/8½ fl oz) water. Bring to the boil, then reduce the heat and simmer for 30 minutes. Season to taste.

3 Meanwhile, slice the bread into four thick slices and arrange them in a single layer under a hot grill (broiler). Toast one side, turn and sprinkle with Parmesan, and toast until crisp and golden and the cheese has melted.

4 Put the bread slices into serving bowls. Ladle in the hot soup, sprinkle with the cheese and parsley and serve.

ASIAN CHICKEN NOODLE SOUP

Preparation time:
10 minutes

Total cooking time:
10 minutes

Serves 4

INGREDIENTS

- 85 g (3 oz) fresh egg noodles
- 1.25 litres (1.3 US qt/1.1 UK qt) chicken stock (broth)
- 1 tablespoon mirin (see NOTE)
- 2 tablespoons soy sauce
- 3 cm (1¼ inch) piece fresh ginger (gingerroot), julienned
- 2 chicken breast fillets, thinly sliced
- 2 bunches baby bok choy, leaves separated
- fresh coriander (cilantro) leaves, to garnish

1 Soak the noodles in boiling water for 1 minute, then drain and set aside. In a large saucepan, heat the stock (broth) to simmering, and add the mirin, soy sauce, ginger (gingerroot), chicken and noodles. Cook for 5 minutes, or until the chicken is tender and the noodles are warmed through. Remove any scum from the surface of the soup.

2 Add the bok choy and cook for a further 2 minutes, or until the bok choy leaves have wilted. Serve in deep bowls, garnished with fresh coriander (cilantro) leaves. Serve with sweet chilli sauce, if desired.

NOTE: Mirin is a sweet rice wine used for cooking. Sweet sherry, with a little sugar added, can be used instead.

SPICY VIETNAMESE BEEF AND PORK NOODLE SOUP

Preparation time:
20 minutes +
30 minutes freezing

Total cooking time:
40 minutes

Serves 4

INGREDIENTS

- 300 g (10½ oz) beef fillet steak
- ¼ cup (60 ml/2 fl oz) vegetable oil
- 300 g (10½ oz) pork leg fillet, cut into 3 cm (1¼ inch) cubes
- 1 large onion, cut into thin wedges
- 2 litres (2.1 US qt/1.75 UK qt) good-quality beef stock (broth)
- 2 stems lemongrass
- 2 tablespoons fish sauce
- 1 teaspoon ground dried shrimp
- 1 teaspoon sugar

- 2 large fresh red chillies, sliced
- 400 g (14 oz) fresh round rice noodles
- 2 cups (180 g/6⅓ oz) bean sprouts, tailed
- ½ cup (10 g/⅓ oz) fresh mint
- ½ cup (15 g/½ oz) fresh coriander (cilantro) leaves
- thinly sliced fresh chilli, to serve (optional)
- lemon wedges, to serve

1 Place the beef in the freezer for 20–30 minutes, or until partially frozen, then cut into paper-thin slices across the grain. Set aside.

2 Heat a wok until hot, add 1 tablespoon of the oil and swirl to coat the side of the wok.

Stir-fry (scramble-fry) the pork in batches for 2–3 minutes, or until browned. Remove from the wok. Add another tablespoon of oil and stir-fry (scramble-fry) the onion for 2–3 minutes, or until softened.

3 Pour in the stock (broth) and 2 cups (500 ml / 17 fl oz) water. Bruise one of the lemongrass stems and add it to the wok. Return the pork to the wok and bring the liquid to the boil, then reduce the heat and simmer for 15 minutes, or until the pork is tender, periodically skimming off any scum that rises to the surface. Meanwhile, thinly slice the white part of the remaining lemongrass stem.

4 Remove the whole lemongrass stem from the broth and stir in the fish sauce, dried shrimp and sugar and keep at a simmer.

5 Heat the remaining oil in a small frying pan over medium heat and cook the sliced lemongrass and chilli for 2–3 minutes, or until fragrant. Stir into the broth. Just before serving, bring the broth to the boil over medium–high heat.

6 Place the rice noodles in a large heatproof bowl, cover with boiling water and gently separate the noodles. Drain immediately and rinse. Divide the noodles among four warm serving bowls. Top with the bean sprouts and cover with the boiling broth. Add the beef to the soup – the heat of the soup will cook it. Sprinkle with the mint and coriander (cilantro), and fresh chilli, if desired. Serve immediately with some wedges of lemon.

SOUPE DE POISSON

Preparation time:
30 minutes

Total cooking time:
45 minutes

Serves 6

INGREDIENTS

- 1 large ripe tomato
- 1½ kg (3 lb 5 oz) chopped fish bones from white-fleshed fish
- 1 leek, white part only, chopped
- 1 carrot, chopped
- 1 stick (rib) celery, chopped
- 1 large clove garlic, chopped
- 1 bay leaf
- 3 fresh parsley stalks
- 6 black peppercorns
- 1 cup (250 ml/8½ fl oz) dry white wine
- 1 tablespoon lemon juice
- 250 g (8¾ oz) skinless fish fillets (eg. snapper, perch, cod, red mullet), cut into bite-sized pieces
- 2 tablespoons chervil leaves
- ¼ lemon, cut into very fine slices

1 Score a cross in the base of the tomato. Place in a heatproof bowl and cover with boiling water. Leave for 30 seconds, transfer to cold water, drain and peel away from the cross. Cut the tomato in half, scoop out the seeds with a teaspoon and finely chop the flesh.

2 Rinse the bones well in cold water and combine in a large pan with the leek, carrot, celery, garlic, bay leaf, parsley, peppercorns, wine, lemon juice and 2 litres (2.1 US qt/1.75 UK qt) water. Slowly bring to the boil, skimming off any scum that forms on the surface. Reduce the heat and simmer for 20 minutes.

3 Strain and discard the fish and vegetables. Strain the soup again, through a sieve lined with dampened muslin, into a clean pan. Simmer, uncovered, for 10 minutes.

4 Add the fish pieces and simmer for 2 minutes, or until tender. Season, to taste, with salt and ground white pepper.

5 Divide the chopped tomato and chervil among six warm bowls and ladle the hot soup over them. Float lemon slices on top and serve immediately.

HOT AND SOUR LIME SOUP WITH BEEF

Preparation time:
20 minutes

Total cooking time:
35 minutes

Serves 4

INGREDIENTS

- 1 litre (1.1 US qt/1.75 UK pt) beef stock (broth)
- 2 stems lemongrass, white part only, halved
- 3 cloves garlic, halved
- 2.5 cm × 2.5 cm (1 inch × 1 inch) piece fresh ginger (gingerroot), sliced
- 95 g (3⅓ oz) fresh coriander (cilantro), leaves and stalks separated
- Two 1.5 cm × 4 cm (⅝ inch × 1½ inch) strips lime rind
- 2 star anise

- 3 small fresh red chillies, seeded and finely chopped
- 4 spring (green) onions, thinly sliced on the diagonal
- 500 g (1 lb 2 oz) beef fillet steak, trimmed
- 2 tablespoons fish sauce
- 1 tablespoon grated palm sugar
- 2 tablespoons lime juice
- fresh coriander (cilantro) leaves, extra, to garnish

1 Place stock (broth), lemongrass, garlic ginger (gingerroot), coriander (cilantro) stalks, rind, star anise, 1 teaspoon chopped chilli, half the spring (green) onion, and 1 litre (1.1 US qt/1.75 UK pt) water in a saucepan. Bring to the boil and simmer, covered, for 25 minutes. Strain and return the liquid to the pan.

2 Heat a chargrill (charbroil) pan until very hot. Brush with olive oil and sear the steak on both sides until browned on the outside, but very rare in the centre.

3 Reheat soup, adding the fish sauce and palm sugar. Season and add the lime juice to taste (you may want more than 2 tablespoons) — you should achieve a hot and sour flavour.

4 Add the remaining spring (green) onion and the chopped coriander (cilantro) leaves to the soup. Slice the beef across the grain into thin strips. Curl the strips into a decorative pattern, then place in four deep serving bowls. Pour the soup over the beef and garnish with the chilli and coriander (cilantro).

TOMATO DITALINI SOUP

Preparation time:
15 minutes

Total cooking time:
20 minutes

Serves 4

INGREDIENTS

- 2 tablespoons olive oil
- 1 large onion, finely chopped
- 2 celery sticks (ribs), finely chopped
- 3 vine-ripened tomatoes
- 1.5 litres (1.6 US qt/1.3 UK qt) chicken or vegetable stock (broth)
- ½ cup (90 g/3¼ oz) ditalini pasta
- 2 tablespoons chopped fresh flat-leaf parsley

1 Heat the oil in a large saucepan over medium heat. Add the onion and celery and cook for 5 minutes, or until they have softened.

2 Score a cross in the base of each tomato, then place them in a bowl of boiling water for 1 minute. Plunge into cold water and peel the skin away from the cross. Halve the tomatoes and scoop out the seeds. Roughly chop the flesh. Add the stock (broth) and tomato to the onion mixture and bring to the boil. Add the pasta and cook for 10 minutes, or until *al dente*. Season and sprinkle with parsley. Serve with crusty bread.

SEAFOOD RAVIOLI
IN GINGERY SOUP

Preparation time:	**Total cooking time:**	**Serves** 4
30 minutes	20 minutes	

INGREDIENTS

- 8 raw prawns (shrimp)
- 1 carrot, chopped
- 1 onion, chopped
- 1 celery stick (rib), chopped
- 3 spring (green) onions, thinly sliced
- 6 cm (2½ inch) piece fresh ginger (gingerroot), thinly shredded
- 1 tablespoon mirin (sweet rice wine)
- 1 teaspoon kecap manis (Indonesian soy sauce)

- 1 tablespoon soy sauce
- 4 large scallops
- 100 g (3½ oz) boneless white fish fillet
- 1 egg white
- 200 g (7 oz) round gow gee wrappers
- ⅓ cup (10 g/⅓ oz) fresh coriander (cilantro) leaves

1 To make the soup, peel the prawns (shrimp), reserve 4 for the ravioli filling and chop the rest into small pieces and reserve. Put the prawn (shrimp) heads and shells in a large pan, cook over high heat until starting to brown, then cover with 1 litre (1.1 US qt/1.75 UK pt) water. Add the carrot, onion and celery, bring to the boil, reduce the heat and simmer for 10 minutes. Strain and discard the prawn (shrimp) heads, shells and vegetables. Return the stock (broth) to a clean pan and add the spring (green) onion, ginger (gingerroot), mirin, kecap manis (Indonesian soy sauce) and soy sauce. Set aside.

2 To make the ravioli, chop the whole reserved prawns (shrimp) with the scallops and fish in a food processor until smooth. Add enough egg white to bind. Lay half the gow gee wrappers on a work surface and place a rounded teaspoon of filling in the centre of each. Brush the edges with water. Top each with another wrapper and press the edges to seal, eliminating air bubbles as you go. Trim with a fluted cutter. Cover with plastic wrap.

3 Bring a large pan of water to the boil. Meanwhile, heat the stock (broth) and leave simmering. Just prior to serving, drop a few ravioli at a time into the boiling water. Cook for 2 minutes, remove with a slotted spoon and divide among heated bowls. Cook the chopped reserved prawns (shrimp) in the same water for 2 minutes; drain. Pour the hot stock (broth) over the ravioli and serve, sprinkled with the chopped cooked prawns (shrimp) and coriander (cilantro) leaves.

ROAST DUCK AND NOODLE BROTH

Preparation time:
25 minutes + 25 minutes soaking

Total cooking time:
10 minutes

Serves 4–6

INGREDIENTS

- 3 dried shiitake mushrooms
- 1 Chinese roast duck
  (1.5 kg/3 lb 5 oz)
- 2 cups (500 ml/17 fl oz) chicken
  stock (broth)
- 2 tablespoons light soy sauce
- 1 tablespoon Chinese rice wine
- 2 teaspoons sugar
- 400 g (14 oz) fresh flat rice noodles
- 2 tablespoons oil
- 3 spring (green) onions,
  thinly sliced
- 1 teaspoon finely chopped fresh
  ginger (gingerroot)
- 400 g (14 oz) bok choy,
  leaves separated
- ¼ teaspoon sesame oil

1 Soak the mushrooms in 1 cup
(250 ml/8½ fl oz) boiling water
for 20 minutes. Drain, reserving
the liquid and squeezing
the excess liquid from the
mushrooms. Discard the stems
and thinly slice the caps.

2 Remove the skin and flesh from
the duck. Discard the fat and
carcass. Finely slice the duck
meat and the skin (you should
have about 400 g/14 oz of
duck meat).

3 Place the chicken stock (broth),
soy sauce, rice wine, sugar and
the reserved mushroom liquid in
a saucepan over medium heat.
Bring to a simmer and cook for
5 minutes.

4 Meanwhile, place the rice
noodles in a heatproof bowl,
cover with boiling water and
soak briefly. Gently separate the
noodles with your hands and
drain well. Divide evenly among
large soup bowls.

5 Heat the oil in a wok over high heat. Add the spring (green) onion, ginger (gingerroot) and mushrooms, and cook for several seconds. Transfer to the broth with the bok choy and duck meat, and simmer for 1 minute, or until the duck has warmed through and the bok choy has wilted. Ladle the soup on the noodles and drizzle sesame oil on each serving. Serve immediately.

PORK, CORN AND NOODLE SOUP

Preparation time:
15 minutes

Total cooking time:
30 minutes

Serves 4

INGREDIENTS

- 2 small fresh corn cobs
- 200 g (7 oz) dried ramen noodles
- 2 teaspoons peanut oil
- 1 teaspoon grated fresh ginger (gingerroot)
- 1.5 litres (1.6 US qt / 1.3 UK qt) chicken stock (broth)
- 2 tablespoons mirin (sweet rice wine)
- 200 g (7 oz) piece Chinese barbecued pork (char sui), thinly sliced
- 3 spring (green) onions, sliced on the diagonal
- 20 g (⅔ oz) unsalted butter

1 Remove the corn kernels from the cob using a sharp knife.

2 Cook the ramen noodles in a large saucepan of boiling water for 4 minutes, or until tender. Drain, then rinse in cold water.

3 Heat the oil in a large saucepan over high heat. Stir-fry (scramble-fry) the ginger (gingerroot) for 1 minute. Add the chicken stock (broth) and mirin and bring to the boil. Reduce the heat and simmer for 8 minutes.

4 Add the pork slices and cook for 5 minutes, then add the corn kernels and two-thirds of the spring (green) onion, and cook for a further 4–5 minutes, or until the corn is tender.

5 Separate the noodles by running them under hot water, then divide them among four deep bowls. Ladle on the soup, then place 1 teaspoon butter on each serving. Garnish with the remaining spring (green) onion and serve immediately.

NOTE: This soup is traditionally served with the butter on top. However, for a healthier option, it is also quite delicious without the butter.

VIETNAMESE FISH AND NOODLE SOUP

Preparation time:
30 minutes + 5 minutes soaking

Total cooking time:
25 minutes

Serves 4

INGREDIENTS

- 1 teaspoon shrimp paste
- 150 g (5¼ oz) mung bean vermicelli (glass or cellophane noodles)
- 2 tablespoons peanut oil
- 6 cloves garlic, finely chopped
- 1 small onion, thinly sliced
- 2 long fresh red chillies, chopped
- 2 stems lemongrass (white part only), thinly sliced
- 1.25 litres (1.3 US qt/1.1 UK qt) chicken stock (broth)
- ¼ cup (60 ml/2 fl oz) fish sauce
- 1 tablespoon rice vinegar
- 4 ripe tomatoes, peeled, seeded and chopped

- 500 g (1 lb 2 oz) firm white fish fillets (snapper or blue-eye), cut into 3 cm (1¼ inch) pieces
- ½ cup (10 g/⅓ oz) fresh Vietnamese mint, torn
- ½ cup (15 g/½ oz) fresh coriander (cilantro) leaves
- 1 cup (90 g/3¼ oz) bean sprouts
- 1 tablespoon fresh Vietnamese mint, extra
- 1 tablespoon fresh coriander (cilantro) leaves, extra
- 2 long fresh red chillies, extra, sliced
- lemon wedges, to serve

1 Wrap the shrimp paste in foil and place it under a hot grill (broiler) for 1 minute. Remove and set aside until needed.

2 Soak the vermicelli (noodles) in boiling water for 3–4 minutes. Rinse under cold water, drain and then cut into 15 cm (6 inch) lengths.

3 Heat the oil in a heavy-based
saucepan over medium heat. Add
the garlic and cook for 1 minute,
or until golden. Add the onion,
chilli, lemongrass and shrimp
paste, and cook, stirring, for a
further minute. Pour in the
stock (broth), fish sauce and rice
vinegar, then add the tomato.
Bring to the boil, then reduce the
heat to medium and simmer for

10 minutes. Add the fish and
simmer gently for 3 minutes, or
until cooked. Stir in the mint and
coriander (cilantro) leaves.

4 Divide the noodles and bean
sprouts among four serving
bowls and ladle the soup on top.
Top with the extra mint, coriander
(cilantro) leaves and chilli. Serve
with lemon wedges.

SOBA NOODLE AND VEGETABLE SOUP

Preparation time:
15 minutes + 5 minutes soaking

Total cooking time:
10 minutes

Serves 4

INGREDIENTS

- 250 g (8¾ oz) soba noodles
- 2 dried shiitake mushrooms
- 2 litres (2.1 US qt/1.75 UK qt) vegetable stock (broth)
- 120 g (4¼ oz) snow peas (mange tout), cut into thin strips
- 2 small carrots, cut into thin 5 cm (2 inch) strips
- 2 cloves garlic, finely chopped
- 6 spring (green) onions, cut into 5 cm (2 inch) lengths and thinly sliced lengthways
- 3 cm (1¼ inch) piece fresh ginger (gingerroot), julienned
- ⅓ cup (80 ml/2¾ fl oz) soy sauce
- ¼ cup (60 ml/2 fl oz) mirin (sweet rice wine) or sake
- 1 cup (90 g/3¼ oz) bean sprouts
- coriander (cilantro), to garnish

1 Cook the noodles according to the packet instructions, then drain.

2 Soak the mushrooms in ½ cup (125 ml/4¼ fl oz) boiling water until soft. Drain, reserving the liquid. Discard the stems and slice the caps.

3 Combine the vegetable stock (broth), mushrooms, reserved liquid, snow peas (mange tout), carrot, garlic, spring (green) onion and ginger (gingerroot) in a large saucepan. Bring slowly to the boil, then reduce the heat to low and simmer for 5 minutes, or until the vegetables are tender. Add the soy sauce, mirin and bean sprouts. Cook for a further 3 minutes.

4 Divide the noodles among four large serving bowls. Ladle the hot liquid and vegetables over the top and garnish with coriander (cilantro).

SPICY CHICKEN BROTH WITH PASTA

Preparation time:
1 hour

Total cooking time:
50 minutes

Serves 4

INGREDIENTS

- 350 g (12¼ oz) chicken thighs or wings, skin removed
- 2 carrots, finely chopped
- 2 celery sticks (ribs), finely chopped
- 2 small leeks, finely chopped
- 3 egg whites
- 6 cups (1.5 litres/1.6 US qt/ 1.3 UK qt) chicken stock (broth)
- hot chilli (pepper) sauce

PASTA
- ½ cup (60 g/2 oz) plain (all-purpose) flour
- 1 egg
- ½ teaspoon sesame oil
- 90 g (3¼ oz) coriander (cilantro) leaves

1 Put the chicken pieces, carrot, celery and leek in a large heavy-based pan. Push the chicken to one side and add the egg whites to the vegetables. Using a wire whisk, beat for a minute or so, until frothy (take care not to use a pan that can be scratched by the whisk).

2 Warm the stock (broth) in another pan, then add gradually to the first pan, whisking continuously to froth the egg whites. Continue whisking while slowly bringing to the boil. Make a hole in the froth on top with a spoon and leave to simmer for 30 minutes, without stirring.

3 Line a large strainer with a damp tea towel or double thickness of muslin and strain the broth into a clean bowl (discard the chicken and vegetables). Season with salt, pepper and hot chilli (pepper) sauce, to taste. Set aside until you are ready to serve.

4 To make the pasta, sift the flour into a bowl and make a well in the centre. Whisk the egg and oil together and pour into the well. Mix together to make a soft pasta dough and knead on a lightly floured surface for 2 minutes, until smooth.

5 Divide the pasta dough into four even portions. Roll one portion out very thinly and cover with a layer of evenly spaced coriander (cilantro) leaves. Roll out another portion of pasta and lay this on top of the leaves, then gently roll the layers together. Repeat with the remaining pasta and coriander (cilantro).

6 Cut out squares of pasta around the leaves. The pasta may then be left to sit and dry out if it is not needed immediately. When you are ready to serve, heat the chicken broth gently in a pan. As the broth simmers, add the pasta and cook for 1 minute. Serve immediately.

NOTE: The egg whites added to the vegetable and chicken stock (broth) make the broth very clear, rather than leaving it with the normal cloudy appearance of chicken stock (broth). This is called clarifying the stock (broth). When you strain the broth through muslin or a tea towel, don't press the solids to extract the extra liquid or the broth will become cloudy. It is necessary to make a hole in the froth on top to prevent the stock (broth) boiling over.

CHINESE PORK AND NOODLE SOUP

Preparation time:
25 minutes + overnight
refrigeration + 1 hour
refrigeration

Total cooking time:
4 hours

Serves 4–6

INGREDIENTS

STOCK (BROTH)
- 1.5 kg (3 lb 5 oz) chicken bones
  (chicken necks, backs, wings), washed
- 3 cloves garlic, sliced
- 2 slices fresh ginger (gingerroot),
  1 cm (½ inch) thick
- 4 spring (green) onions, white part only

- 150 g (5¼ oz) Chinese cabbage,
  shredded
- 1 tablespoon peanut oil
- 2 teaspoons sesame oil
- 4 cloves garlic, crushed

- 1 tablespoon grated fresh
  ginger (gingerroot)
- 300 g (10½ oz) pork mince
  (ground pork)
- 1 egg white
- ¼ teaspoon ground white pepper
- 2 tablespoons light soy sauce
- 1 tablespoon Chinese rice wine
- 1½ tablespoons cornflour (cornstarch)
- ½ cup (15 g/½ oz) fresh coriander
  (cilantro) leaves, finely chopped
- 6 spring (green) onions, thinly sliced
- 200 g (7 oz) fresh thin egg noodles

1 To make the stock (broth),
   place the bones and 3.5 litres
   (3.7 US qt/3.1 UK qt) water in
   a large saucepan and bring to a
   simmer – do not boil. Cook for
   30 minutes, removing any scum
   that rises to the surface. Add the
   garlic, ginger (gingerroot) and

   spring (green) onion, and cook,
   partially covered, at a low
   simmer for 3 hours. Strain
   through a fine sieve, then cool.
   Cover and refrigerate overnight.
   Remove the layer of fat from the
   surface once it has solidified.

2 Bring a large saucepan of water to the boil and cook the cabbage for 2 minutes, or until soft. Drain, cool and squeeze out the excess water.

3 Heat the peanut oil and 1 teaspoon of the sesame oil in a small frying pan, and cook the garlic and ginger (gingerroot) for 1 minute, or until the garlic just starts to brown. Allow to cool.

4 Combine the mince (ground pork), cabbage, garlic mixture, egg white, white pepper, soy sauce, rice wine, cornflour (cornstarch), half the coriander (cilantro) and half the spring (green) onion. Cover and refrigerate for 1 hour. Shape tablespoons of the mixture into balls.

5 Bring 1.5 litres (1.6 US qt/ 1.3 UK qt) of the stock (broth — freeze the leftover stock/broth) to the boil in a wok over high heat. Reduce the heat to medium and simmer for 1–2 minutes. Add the pork balls and cook, covered, for 8–10 minutes, or until they rise to the surface and are cooked through.

6 Bring a large saucepan of water to the boil. Cook the noodles for 1 minute, then drain and rinse. Divide among serving bowls and ladle the soup and balls on top. Garnish with the remaining spring (green) onion, coriander (cilantro) and sesame oil.

CLEAR SOUP WITH SALMON QUENELLES

Preparation time:
20 minutes

Total cooking time:
25 minutes

Serves 6

INGREDIENTS

- 400 g (14 oz) salmon cutlets
- 1 litre (1.1 US qt/1.75 UK qt) fish stock (broth)
- ½ cup (125 ml/4¼ fl oz) dry white wine
- 2 teaspoons lemon juice
- 1 small carrot, finely chopped
- 2 spring (green) onions, sliced
- 2 sprigs fresh dill (dill weed)
- 2 sprigs fresh parsley
- 3 black peppercorns
- 1 egg white, well chilled
- ½ cup (125 ml/4¼ fl oz) cream, well chilled
- 2 tablespoons fresh chervil leaves

1 Remove the skin and bones from the salmon and set aside. For the quenelles, weigh 150 g (5¼ oz) of the fish, chop roughly, cover and chill well. For the soup, in a large pan, combine the skin and bones with the remaining salmon, fish stock (broth), wine, lemon juice, carrot, spring (green) onion, dill (dill weed), parsley and peppercorns. Slowly bring to the boil, then reduce the heat, cover and simmer for 15 minutes. Strain and discard the vegetables. (You won't be using the cooked salmon for this recipe, but you can use it as a sandwich filling.)

2 Pour the soup into a clean pan, bring to the boil, then reduce the heat to just simmering. Season, to taste.

3 To make the quenelles, process the reserved salmon in a food processor until finely chopped. Gradually add the egg white and process until smooth. Transfer to a chilled bowl and season well with salt and ground white pepper. Whip the cream and quickly fold into the salmon. Shape quenelles using 2 teaspoons dipped in cold water. Add to the soup in two batches and poach for 2 minutes, or until cooked. Transfer the quenelles to warm soup bowls.

4 Heat the soup to almost boiling and carefully ladle over the quenelles. Sprinkle with chervil leaves and serve.

EIGHT-TREASURE NOODLE SOUP

Preparation time:
20 minutes + 20
minutes soaking

Total cooking time:
20 minutes

Serves 4

INGREDIENTS

- 10 g (⅓ oz) dried shiitake mushrooms
- 375 g (13¼ oz) fresh thick egg noodles
- 1.2 litres (1.3 US qt/1.1 UK qt) chicken stock (broth)
- ¼ cup (60 ml/2 fl oz) light soy sauce
- 2 teaspoons Chinese rice wine
- 200 g (7 oz) chicken breast fillet, cut into 1 cm (½ inch) strips on the diagonal

- 200 g (7 oz) Chinese barbecued pork (char sui), cut into 5 mm (¼ inch) slices
- ¼ onion, finely chopped
- 1 carrot, cut into 1 cm (½ inch) slices on the diagonal
- 120 g (4¼ oz) snow peas (mange tout), cut in half on the diagonal
- 4 spring (green) onions, thinly sliced

1 Soak the mushrooms in boiling water for 20 minutes, or until soft. Drain and squeeze out any excess liquid. Discard the stems and thinly slice the caps.

2 Bring a large saucepan of water to the boil and cook the noodles for 1 minute, or until cooked through. Drain, then rinse with cold water. Divide evenly among four deep, warmed serving bowls.

3 Meanwhile, bring the chicken stock (broth) to the boil in a large saucepan over high heat. Reduce the heat to medium and stir in the soy sauce and rice wine. Simmer for 2 minutes. Add the chicken and pork and cook for 2 minutes, or until the chicken is cooked and the pork is heated through. Add the onion, carrot, snow peas (mange tout), mushrooms and half the spring (green) onion, and cook for 1 minute, or until the carrot is tender.

4 Divide the vegetables and meat among the serving bowls and ladle on the hot broth. Garnish with the remaining spring (green) onion.

MISO WITH RAMEN

Preparation time:
15 minutes + 15 minutes soaking

Total cooking time:
15 minutes

Serves 4

INGREDIENTS

- 1 teaspoon finely chopped dried wakame (edible seaweed)
- 180 g (6⅓ oz) fresh ramen noodles
- 100 g (3½ oz) silken firm tofu, cut into 1.5 cm (⅝ inch) cubes
- 2 spring (green) onions, thinly sliced on the diagonal
- 1¾ teaspoons dashi (Japanese stock) powder
- 2–3 tablespoons red miso (see NOTE)
- 2 teaspoons mirin (sweet rice wine)
- 2 teaspoon Japanese soy sauce

1 Soak the wakame (seaweed) in a bowl of tepid water for 15 minutes. Drain and set aside.

2 Cook the noodles in a large saucepan of boiling salted water for 2 minutes, or until cooked through. Drain and rinse, then divide among warmed serving bowls. Place the tofu and spring (green) onion on top.

3 Meanwhile, bring 1.25 litres (1.3 US qt/1.1 UK qt) water to the boil in a large saucepan. Reduce the heat to low and add the dashi (Japanese stock) powder, stirring for 30 seconds, or until dissolved.

4 In a bowl, combine the miso with 1 cup (250 ml/8½ fl oz) of the dashi stock, whisking until smooth. Return the miso mixture to the pan of stock (broth) and stir until combined – be careful not to boil the broth as this will diminish the flavour of the miso. Add the mirin, soy sauce and wakame (seaweed), and gently heat for 1 minute, then stir to combine. Ladle the broth over the noodles, tofu and spring (green) onion, and serve immediately.

NOTE: Shiro (white) miso can be used instead of red miso, however, the flavour will not be as strong – adjust to taste.

FISH BALL AND NOODLE SOUP

Preparation time:
20 minutes

Total cooking time:
15 minutes

Serves 4–6

INGREDIENTS

- 500 g (1 lb 2 oz) firm white fish fillets, skin and bones removed (ling or perch)
- 2 tablespoons rice flour
- 200 g (7 oz) dried somen noodles
- 2½ teaspoons dashi (Japanese stock) powder
- 2 tablespoons light soy sauce
- 1 tablespoon mirin (sweet rice wine)
- 200 g (7 oz) Chinese cabbage, shredded
- 2 spring (green) onions, thinly sliced on the diagonal
- ½ Lebanese cucumber, unpeeled, seeded and cut into 5 cm (2 inch) strips

1 Place the fish in a food processor and process until smooth. Combine the rice flour and ⅓ cup (80 ml / 2¾ fl oz) water in a small bowl, and stir until smooth, then add to the fish and process for a further 5 seconds. Using 2 teaspoons of mixture at a time, shape into balls with wet hands.

2 Cook the somen noodles in a large saucepan of boiling water for 2 minutes, or until tender, then drain.

3 Bring 2 litres (2.1 US qt / 1.75 UK qt) water to the boil in a large saucepan. Reduce the heat to low, add the dashi (Japanese stock) powder and stir until dissolved. Bring the stock (broth) to the boil over high heat and add the soy sauce, mirin and salt to taste. Add the fish balls, reduce the heat to medium and simmer for 3 minutes, or until the balls rise to the surface and they are cooked through. Add the cabbage, increase the heat to high and return to the boil. Stir in the noodles and cook for 1 minute, or until warmed through.

4 To serve, divide the noodles and fish balls among serving bowls, then ladle the liquid on top. Garnish with the spring (green) onion and cucumber.

MINESTRONE

Preparation time:
30 minutes

Total cooking time:
2 hours 30 minutes

Serves 8

INGREDIENTS

- 1 tablespoon olive oil
- 1 onion, finely chopped
- 2 cloves garlic, crushed
- 2 carrots, diced
- 2 potatoes, diced
- 2 celery sticks (ribs), finely chopped
- 2 zucchini (courgettes), finely chopped
- 2 cups (150 g/5¼ oz) shredded cabbage

- 125 g (4⅓ oz) green beans, chopped
- 2 litres (2.1 US qt/1.75 UK qt) beef stock (broth)
- 425 g (15 oz) can chopped tomatoes
- ½ cup (80 g/2¾ oz) macaroni
- 440 g (15½ oz) can borlotti (romano) or red kidney beans, drained
- grated Parmesan, to serve
- fresh thyme sprigs, to serve

1 Heat the oil in a large heavy-based pan. Add the onion and garlic and cook over low heat for 5 minutes. Add the carrot, potato and celery and cook, stirring, for a further 5 minutes.

2 Add the zucchini (courgette), cabbage and green beans to the pan and cook, stirring, for 5 minutes. Add the stock (broth) and chopped tomatoes. Bring slowly to the boil, then reduce the heat, cover and leave to simmer for 2 hours.

3 Add the macaroni and beans, and cook for 15 minutes, or until the pasta is tender. Serve hot with a sprinkling of Parmesan and garnished with a sprig of fresh thyme.

NOTE: Any type of pasta can be used for minestrone, though smaller shapes are easier to manage on a soup spoon.

CORN AND CRAB SOUP

Preparation time:
15 minutes

Total cooking time:
10 minutes

Serves 4

INGREDIENTS

- 1½ tablespoons oil
- 6 cloves garlic, chopped
- 6 red Asian shallots, chopped
- 2 stems lemongrass, white part only, finely chopped
- 1 tablespoon grated fresh ginger (gingerroot)
- 1 litre (1.1 US qt/1.75 UK pt) chicken stock (broth)

- 1 cup (250 ml/8½ fl oz) coconut milk
- 2½ cups (375 g/13¼ oz) frozen corn kernels
- 2 × 170 g (6 oz) cans crab meat, drained
- 2 tablespoons fish sauce
- 2 tablespoons lime juice
- 1 teaspoon shaved palm sugar or soft brown sugar

1 Heat the oil in a large saucepan, then add the chopped garlic, shallots and lemongrass and the grated ginger (gingerroot) and cook, stirring, over medium heat for 2 minutes.

2 Pour the chicken stock (broth) and coconut milk into the saucepan and bring to the boil, stirring occasionally. Add the corn kernels and continue to cook for 5 minutes.

3 Add the drained crab meat, fish sauce, lime juice and sugar to the saucepan and stir until the crab is heated through. Season with salt and black pepper, to taste. Ladle into bowls and serve immediately.

OXTAIL SOUP

Preparation time:
20 minutes + chilling

Total cooking time:
3 hours 20 minutes

Serves 4

INGREDIENTS

- 1 tablespoon plain
  (all-purpose) flour
- 1 kg (2 lb 3 oz) oxtail, chopped
  into 5 cm (2 inch) pieces (ask your
  butcher to do this)
- 1 tablespoon oil
- 2 litres (2.1 US qt / 1.75 UK qt)
  beef stock (broth)
- 1 onion, chopped
- 1 celery stick (rib), chopped
- 2 carrots, chopped
- 1 swede (yellow turnip / rutabaga)
  or turnip, peeled and chopped
- 3 whole cloves
- 12 peppercorns
- 2 bay leaves
- 1 tablespoon plain (all-purpose)
  flour, extra
- 2 tablespoons port
- 1 tablespoon tomato paste
  (tomato puree)
- ⅓ cup (20 g / ⅔ oz) finely chopped
  fresh parsley

1 Season the flour, put it in a plastic
  bag with the oxtail and shake to
  coat. Shake off excess flour. Heat
  the oil in a large pan, add the
  oxtail and cook in batches,
  tossing continually, for 5 minutes,
  or until evenly browned. Return
  all the oxtail to the pan.

2 Add the stock (broth), 1½ cups
  (375 ml / 13 fl oz) water,
  vegetables, cloves, peppercorns,
  bay leaves and ½ teaspoon salt.
  Bring slowly to the boil then
  reduce the heat and simmer,
  covered, for 3 hours.

3 Strain the vegetables and meat,
  reserving the liquid. Discard the
  vegetables and leave the meat
  to cool. Pull the meat from the
  bone, shred and refrigerate.
  Meanwhile, refrigerate the
  stock (broth) until the fat has
  solidified on the surface and can
  be removed with a spoon. Add
  the meat.

4 Put the soup in a clean pan. Mix
  together the extra flour, port and
  tomato paste (tomato puree), and
  add to the pan. Bring to the boil,
  stirring, until the soup thickens
  slightly. Simmer for 10 minutes,
  then stir in the parsley.

CREAMY SEAFOOD BISQUE

Preparation time:
25 minutes

Total cooking time:
25 minutes

Serves 4–6

INGREDIENTS

- 500 g (1 lb 2 oz) raw medium prawns (shrimp)
- 60 g (2 oz) butter
- 2 tablespoons plain (all-purpose) flour
- 2 litres (2.1 US qt/1.75 UK qt) fish stock (broth)
- ½ teaspoon paprika
- 1 cup (250 ml/8½ fl oz) cream
- ⅓ cup (80 ml/2¾ fl oz) dry sherry
- 1–2 tablespoons cream, extra, for serving
- paprika, extra, optional, to garnish

1 Peel the prawns (shrimp) and gently pull out the dark vein from each back, starting at the head end. Reserve the heads and shells. Melt the butter in a saucepan, add the prawn (shrimp) heads and shells and cook, stirring, over medium heat for 5 minutes, lightly crushing the heads with a wooden spoon.

2 Add the flour to the saucepan and stir until combined. Add the fish stock (broth) and paprika and stir until the mixture boils. Reduce the heat and simmer, covered, over low heat for 10 minutes. Strain the mixture through a fine sieve set over a bowl, then return the liquid to the saucepan. Discard the shells. Add the prawns (shrimp) to the saucepan and cook over low heat for 2–3 minutes. Cool slightly, then process in batches in a blender or food processor until smooth. Return to the saucepan.

3 Add the cream and sherry to the pan and stir to heat through. Season, to taste, with salt and freshly ground black pepper. Serve topped with a swirl of cream and sprinkled with paprika, if desired.

NOTE: A few of the small cooked prawns (shrimp) can be reserved for garnishing.

CHICKEN AND COCONUT MILK SOUP

Preparation time:
30 minutes +
5 minutes soaking

Total cooking time:
15 minutes

Serves 8

INGREDIENTS

- 150 g (5¼ oz) dried rice vermicelli
- 1 lime
- 4 small fresh red chillies, seeded and chopped
- 1 medium onion, chopped
- 2 cloves garlic, crushed
- 4 thin slices fresh ginger (gingerroot), finely chopped
- 2 stems lemongrass (white part only), chopped
- 1 tablespoon chopped fresh coriander (cilantro)

- 1 tablespoon peanut oil
- 3 cups (750 ml/26 fl oz) chicken stock (broth)
- 2¾ cups (685 ml/24 fl oz) coconut milk
- 500 g (1 lb 2 oz) chicken tenderloins, cut into thin strips
- 4 spring (green) onions, chopped
- 150 g (5¼ oz) fried tofu puffs, sliced
- 1 cup (90 g/3¼ oz) bean sprouts
- 3 teaspoons soft brown sugar

1 Soak the vermicelli in boiling water for 5 minutes. Drain, cut into short lengths and set aside.

2 Remove the lime rind with a vegetable peeler and cut it into strips.

3 Place the chilli, onion, garlic, ginger (gingerroot), lemongrass and coriander (cilantro) into a food processor and process in short bursts for 20 seconds, or until smooth.

4 Heat the oil in a large heavy-based saucepan over medium heat. Add the chilli mixture and cook, stirring frequently, for 3 minutes, or until fragrant. Add the stock (broth), coconut milk and lime rind, and bring to the boil. Add the chicken and cook, stirring, for 4 minutes, or until tender.

5 Add the spring (green) onion, tofu, bean sprouts and brown sugar, and season with salt. Stir over medium heat for 3 minutes, or until the spring (green) onion is tender. Divide the noodles among bowls and pour the soup over the top. Garnish with chilli and coriander (cilantro).

PASTA AND BEAN SOUP

Preparation time:
15 minutes +
overnight soaking +
10 minutes resting

Total cooking time:
1 hour 45 minutes

Serves 4

INGREDIENTS

- 200 g (7 oz) dried borlotti (romano) beans
- ¼ cup (60 ml/2 fl oz) olive oil
- 90 g (3¼ oz) piece pancetta, finely diced
- 1 onion, finely chopped
- 2 cloves garlic, crushed
- 1 celery stick (rib), thinly sliced
- 1 carrot, diced
- 1 bay leaf
- 1 sprig fresh rosemary

- 1 sprig fresh flat-leaf parsley
- 400 g (14 oz) can diced tomatoes, drained
- 1.6 litres (1.7 UK qt/1.4 UK qt) vegetable stock (broth)
- 2 tablespoons finely chopped fresh flat-leaf parsley
- 150 g (5¼ oz) ditalini or other small dried pasta
- extra virgin olive oil, to serve
- grated fresh Parmesan, to serve

1 Place the beans in a large bowl, cover with cold water and leave to soak overnight. Drain and rinse.

2 Heat the oil in a large saucepan, add the pancetta, onion, garlic, celery and carrot, and cook over medium heat for 5 minutes, or until golden. Season with pepper.

Add the bay leaf, rosemary, parsley, tomato, stock (broth) and beans, and bring to the boil. Reduce the heat and simmer for 1½ hours, or until the beans are tender. Add more boiling water if necessary to maintain the liquid level.

3 Discard the bay leaf, rosemary and parsley sprigs. Scoop out 1 cup (250 ml / 8½ fl oz) of the bean mixture and puree in a food processor or blender. Return to the pan, season with salt and ground black pepper, and add the parsley and pasta. Simmer for 6 minutes, or until the pasta is al dente. Remove from the heat and set aside for 10 minutes. Serve drizzled with extra virgin olive oil and sprinkled with Parmesan.

NOTE: If you prefer, you can use three 400 g (14 oz) cans drained borlotti (romano) beans. Simmer with the other vegetables for 30 minutes.

CHICKEN LAKSA

Preparation time:
30 minutes +
6–7 minutes soaking

Total cooking time:
35 minutes

Serves 4–6

INGREDIENTS

- 1½ tablespoons coriander seeds
- 1 tablespoon cumin seeds
- 1 teaspoon ground turmeric
- 1 onion, roughly chopped
- 1 tablespoon roughly chopped fresh ginger (gingerroot)
- 3 cloves garlic, peeled
- 3 stems lemongrass (white part only), sliced
- 6 candlenuts or macadamias (see NOTES)
- 4–6 small fresh red chillies
- 2–3 teaspoons shrimp paste, roasted (see NOTES)
- 1 litre (1.1 US qt/1.75 UK qt) chicken stock (broth)
- ¼ cup (60 ml/2 fl oz) oil

- 400 g (14 oz) chicken thigh fillets, cut into 2 cm (¾ inch) pieces
- 3 cups (750 ml/26 fl oz) coconut milk
- 4 fresh kaffir lime leaves
- 2½ tablespoons lime juice
- 2 tablespoons fish sauce
- 2 tablespoons grated palm sugar or soft brown sugar
- 250 g (8¾ oz) dried rice vermicelli
- 1 cup (90 g/3¼ oz) bean sprouts
- 4 fried tofu puffs, julienned
- ¼ cup (15 g/½ oz) roughly chopped fresh Vietnamese mint
- ⅔ cup (20 g/⅔ oz) fresh coriander (cilantro) leaves
- lime wedges, to serve

1 Dry-fry the coriander and cumin seeds in a frying pan over medium heat for 1–2 minutes, or until fragrant, tossing constantly to prevent them burning. Grind finely in a mortar and pestle or a spice grinder.

2 Place all the spices, onion, ginger (gingerroot), garlic, lemongrass, candlenuts, red chillies and shrimp paste in a food processor or blender. Add about ½ cup (125 ml/4¼ fl oz) of the stock (broth) and blend to a fine paste.

3 Heat the oil in a wok or large saucepan over low heat and gently cook the paste for 3–5 minutes, stirring constantly to prevent it burning or sticking to the bottom. Add the remaining stock (broth) and bring to the boil over high heat. Reduce the heat to medium and simmer for 15 minutes, or until reduced slightly. Add the chicken and simmer for 4–5 minutes, or until cooked through.

4 Add the coconut milk, lime leaves, lime juice, fish sauce and palm sugar, and simmer for 5 minutes over medium–low heat. Do not bring to the boil or cover with a lid, as the coconut milk will separate.

5 Meanwhile, place the vermicelli in a heatproof bowl, cover with boiling water and soak for 6–7 minutes, or until softened. Drain and divide among large serving bowls with the bean sprouts. Ladle the hot soup over the top and garnish with some tofu strips, mint and coriander (cilantro) leaves. Serve with a wedge of lime.

NOTES: Raw candlenuts are slightly toxic so must be cooked before use.

To roast the shrimp paste, wrap the paste in foil and place under a hot grill (broiler) for 1 minute.

AVGOLEMONO WITH CHICKEN

Preparation time:
30 minutes

Total cooking time:
30 minutes

Serves 4

INGREDIENTS

- 1 onion, halved
- 2 cloves
- 1 carrot, cut into chunks
- 1 bay leaf
- 500 g (1 lb 2 oz) chicken breast fillets

- ⅓ cup (75 g/2⅔ oz) short-grain rice
- 3 eggs, separated
- ¼ cup (60 ml/2 fl oz) lemon juice
- 2 tablespoons chopped fresh flat-leaf parsley
- 4 thin lemon slices, to garnish

1 Stud the onion halves with the cloves and place in a large saucepan with 1.5 litres (1.6 US qt/1.3 UK qt) water. Add the carrot, bay leaf and chicken. Season with salt and freshly ground black pepper. Slowly bring to the boil, then reduce the heat and simmer for 10 minutes, or until the chicken is cooked.

2 Strain the stock (broth) into a clean saucepan, reserving the chicken and discarding the vegetables. Add the rice to the stock (broth), bring to the boil,

then reduce the heat and simmer for 15 minutes, or until tender. Tear the chicken into shreds.

3 Whisk the egg whites until stiff peaks form, then beat in the yolks. Slowly beat in the lemon juice. Gently stir in 150 ml (5 fl oz) of the hot (not boiling) soup and beat thoroughly. Add the egg mixture to the soup and stir gently over low heat until thickened slightly. It should still be quite thin. Do not let it boil or the eggs may scramble. Add the shredded chicken, and season.

4 Set aside for 3–4 minutes to allow the flavours to develop, then sprinkle with the parsley.

Garnish with the lemon slices and serve immediately.

DUMPLING SOUP

Preparation time: 30 minutes

Total cooking time: 35 minutes

Serves 4

INGREDIENTS

- 1 tablespoon oil
- 1 onion, chopped
- 2 cloves garlic, crushed
- 2 teaspoons ground cumin
- 1 teaspoon ground coriander
- ¼ teaspoon chilli powder
- 2 × 300 g (10½ oz) cans chickpeas (garbanzo beans), drained
- 3½ cups (875 ml/30 fl oz) vegetable stock (broth)
- 2 × 425 g (15 oz) cans chopped tomatoes
- 1 tablespoon chopped fresh coriander (cilantro) leaves
- 1 cup (125 g/4⅓ oz) self-raising flour
- 25 g (¾ oz) butter, chopped
- 2 tablespoons grated fresh Parmesan
- 2 tablespoons mixed chopped fresh herbs (chives, flat-leaf parsley and coriander/cilantro leaves)
- ¼ cup (60 ml/2 fl oz) milk

1 Heat the oil in a large saucepan and cook the onion over medium heat for 2–3 minutes, or until soft. Add the garlic, cumin, ground coriander and chilli, and cook for 1 minute, or until fragrant. Add the chickpeas (garbanzo beans), stock (broth) and tomato. Bring to the boil, then reduce the heat and simmer, covered, for 10 minutes. Stir in the coriander (cilantro).

2 To make the dumplings, sift the flour into a bowl and add the chopped butter. Rub the butter into the flour with your fingertips until it resembles fine breadcrumbs. Stir in the cheese and mixed fresh herbs. Make a well in the centre, add the milk and mix with a flat-bladed knife until just combined. Bring the dough together into a rough ball, divide into eight portions and roll into small balls.

3 Add the dumplings to the soup, cover and simmer for 20 minutes, or until a skewer comes out clean when inserted into the centre of the dumplings.

SEAFOOD LAKSA

Preparation time:
45 minutes

Total cooking time:
50 minutes

Serves 4

INGREDIENTS

- 1 kg (2 lb 3 oz) raw medium prawns (shrimp)
- ⅓ cup (80 ml/2¾ fl oz) oil
- 2–6 small fresh red chillies, seeded
- 1 onion, roughly chopped
- 3 cloves garlic, halved
- 2 cm × 2 cm (¾ inch × ¾ inch) piece fresh ginger (gingerroot) or galangal (Thai ginger), chopped
- 3 stems lemongrass (white part only), chopped
- 1 teaspoon ground turmeric
- 1 tablespoon ground coriander
- 2 teaspoons shrimp paste

- 2½ cups (625 ml/21 fl oz) coconut cream
- 2 teaspoons grated palm sugar or soft brown sugar
- 4 fresh kaffir lime leaves, crushed
- 1–2 tablespoons fish sauce
- 200 g (7 oz) packet fish balls
- 190 g (6¾ oz) packet fried tofu puffs
- 250 g (8¾ oz) dried rice vermicelli
- 125 g (4⅓ oz) bean sprouts
- ⅓ cup (20 g/⅔ oz) chopped fresh mint
- 2 teaspoons fresh coriander (cilantro) leaves

1 Peel the prawns (shrimp) and gently pull out the dark vein from each prawn back, starting at the head end. Reserve the heads, shells and tails. Cover and refrigerate the prawn (shrimp) meat.

2 Heat 2 tablespoons of the oil in a wok or large saucepan and add the prawn (shrimp) shells and heads. Stir over medium heat for 10 minutes, or until orange, then add 1 litre (1.1 US qt/1.75 UK pt) water. Bring to the boil, then reduce the heat and simmer for 15 minutes. Strain the stock (broth) through a fine sieve, discarding the shells. Clean the pan.

3 Finely chop the chillies (use 2 for mild flavour, increase for hot), onion, garlic, ginger (gingerroot) and lemongrass with the turmeric, coriander and ¼ cup (60 ml/2 fl oz) of the prawn (shrimp) stock in a food processor.

4 Heat the remaining oil in the pan, add the chilli mixture and shrimp paste, and stir over medium heat for 3 minutes, or until fragrant. Pour in the remaining stock (broth) and simmer for 10 minutes. Add the coconut cream, sugar, lime leaves and fish sauce, and simmer for 5 minutes. Add the prawns (shrimp) and simmer for 2 minutes, or until firm and light pink. Add the fish balls and tofu puffs, and simmer gently until just heated through.

5 Soak the rice vermicelli in a bowl of boiling water for 2 minutes, then drain and divide it among serving bowls. Top with the bean sprouts and ladle the soup over the top. Sprinkle with the mint and coriander (cilantro).

SMOKED HADDOCK CHOWDER

Preparation time:	Total cooking time:	Serves 4–6
20 minutes	35 minutes	

INGREDIENTS

- 500 g (1 lb 2 oz) smoked haddock
- 1 potato, diced
- 1 celery stick (rib), diced
- 1 onion, finely chopped
- 50 g (1¾ oz) butter
- 1 rasher bacon, rind removed, finely chopped
- 2 tablespoons plain (all-purpose) flour

- ½ teaspoon dry mustard
- ½ teaspoon Worcestershire sauce
- 1 cup (250 ml/8½ fl oz) milk
- ½ cup (30 g/1 oz) chopped fresh parsley
- ¼ cup (60 ml/2 fl oz) cream (optional)

1 To make the fish stock (broth), put the fish in a frying pan, cover with water and bring to the boil. Reduce the heat and simmer for 8 minutes, or until the fish flakes easily. Drain, reserving the fish stock (broth), then peel, bone and flake the fish.

2 Put the potato, celery and onion in a medium saucepan, and pour over enough of the reserved fish stock (broth) to cover the vegetables. Bring to the boil, then reduce the heat and simmer for 8 minutes, or until the vegetables are tender.

3 Melt the butter in a large saucepan, add the bacon and cook, stirring, for 3 minutes. Add the flour, mustard and Worcestershire sauce, and stir until combined. Cook for 1 minute. Remove from the heat and gradually pour in the milk, stirring continuously until smooth. Return to the heat and stir for 5 minutes, until the mixture comes to the boil and has thickened. Stir in the vegetables and remaining stock (broth), then add the parsley and fish. Simmer over low heat for 5 minutes, or until heated through. Taste for seasoning, and serve with some cream, if desired.

NOTE: Chowder is a thick, hearty soup, made with seafood, fish, vegetables or chicken.

COCONUT AND LEMONGRASS SOUP WITH WON TONS

Preparation time:
30 minutes + overnight
refrigeration

Total cooking time:
1 hour 10 minutes

Serves 4

INGREDIENTS

STOCK (BROTH)
- 1.5 kg (3 lb 5 oz) chicken
  bones, washed
- 1 onion, roughly chopped
- 1 cup (125 g/4⅓ oz) roughly
  chopped celery

WON TONS
- 325 g (11¼ oz) raw small prawns
  (shrimp), peeled and deveined,
  finely chopped
- 2 tablespoons finely chopped fresh
  coriander (cilantro) leaves
- 1 tablespoon shredded fresh Thai basil
- 2 tablespoons finely chopped celery
- 2 spring (green) onions, finely chopped

- 20 won ton wrappers
- 1 egg, lightly beaten

BROTH
- 2 tablespoons tom yam paste
- 3 stems lemongrass, white part only,
  thinly sliced
- 6 fresh kaffir lime leaves
- 2 small fresh red chillies, finely chopped
- 200 ml (6¾ fl oz) coconut milk
- 1 tablespoon grated palm sugar
- 1 tablespoon lime juice
- 1 tablespoon fish sauce
- fresh coriander (cilantro) leaves,
  to garnish

1 To make the stock (broth),
put the chicken bones, onion,
celery and 3 litres (3.2 US qt/
2.6 UK qt) water in a large
saucepan and bring slowly to a
simmer over medium heat. Skim
off any scum that rises to the
surface. Reduce the heat and
simmer for 1 hour, skimming the
surface when necessary. Strain
the stock (broth) through a fine
sieve and allow to cool. Cover
with plastic wrap and refrigerate
overnight. Remove the layer
of fat from the surface once it
has solidified.

2 To make the won tons, combine the prawn (shrimp) meat, coriander (cilantro), basil, celery and spring (green) onion. Lay the won ton wrappers out on a clean work surface. Place a heaped teaspoon of prawn (shrimp) mixture in the centre of each wrapper. Brush the edge of each wrapper with a little of the beaten egg. Lift the sides up tightly and pinch around the filling to form a pouch. Repeat with the remaining wrappers and filling to make 20 won tons in total. Cover and refrigerate.

3 Heat a wok over medium heat, add the tom yam paste and cook for 10 seconds, or until fragrant. Gradually whisk in 1 litre (1.1 US qt/1.75 UK pt) of the chicken stock (broth) until combined, then bring to the boil over high heat. Reduce the heat to medium, then add the lemongrass, lime leaves, chilli and coconut milk and simmer for 5 minutes. Stir in the sugar, lime juice and fish sauce. Gently add the won tons and simmer for 2 minutes, or until cooked through. Remove the won tons with a slotted spoon and place five in each serving bowl. Ladle the broth into the bowls and garnish with fresh coriander (cilantro) leaves.

NOTE: Freeze the remaining stock (broth).

SPANISH-STYLE RICE, SEAFOOD AND CHORIZO SOUP

Preparation time:
45 minutes

Total cooking time:
45 minutes

Serves 4

INGREDIENTS

- 1 kg (2 lb 3 oz) black mussels
- 1 cup (250 ml/8½ fl oz) dry sherry
- 1 tablespoon olive oil
- 1 red onion, chopped
- 200 g (7 oz) chorizo sausage, thinly sliced on the diagonal
- 4 garlic cloves, crushed
- ½ cup (100 g/3½ oz) long-grain rice
- 400 g (14 oz) tin chopped tomatoes

- 2 litres (2.1 US qt/1.75 UK qt) chicken stock (broth)
- ½ teaspoon saffron threads
- 2 bay leaves
- 1 tablespoon chopped oregano
- 500 g (1 lb 2 oz) raw prawns (shrimp), peeled and deveined, tails intact
- 3 tablespoons chopped flat-leaf (Italian) parsley

1 Scrub the mussels with a stiff brush and pull out the hairy beards. Discard any broken mussels or open ones that don't close when tapped on the bench. Rinse well. Put the mussels in a saucepan with the sherry and cook, covered, over high heat for 3 minutes, or until the mussels have opened. Strain the liquid into a bowl. Discard any unopened mussels. Remove all but 8 mussels from their shells and discard the empty shells.

2 Heat the oil in a large saucepan over medium heat, add the onion and cook for 5 minutes, or until softened but not browned. Add the chorizo and cook for 3–5 minutes, or until browned, then add the garlic and cook for a further 1 minute.

3 Add the rice to the mixture and
   stir to coat with the chorizo
   mixture. Add the reserved
   mussel cooking liquid and cook
   for 1 minute before adding the
   chopped tomatoes, stock (broth),
   saffron, bay leaves and oregano.
   Bring to the boil, then reduce the
   heat and simmer, covered, for
   25 minutes.

4 Add the prawns (shrimp) and the
   mussels (except the ones in their
   shells) to the soup, cover with a
   lid, and cook for 3 minutes, then
   stir in the parsley. Ladle into four
   bowls, then top each bowl with
   2 mussels still in their shells.

RAINBOW CONGEE

Preparation time:
15 minutes + 30 minutes soaking

Total cooking time:
2 hours 15 minutes

Serves 6

INGREDIENTS

* 200 g (7 oz) short-grain rice
* 2 dried Chinese mushrooms
* 85 g (3 oz) snow peas (mange tout), trimmed
* 2 Chinese sausages (lap cheong)
* 2 tablespoons oil
* ¼ red onion, finely diced
* 1 carrot, cut into 1 cm (½ inch) dice
* 2 litres (2.1 US qt/1.75 UK qt) chicken stock (broth) or water
* 3 teaspoons light soy sauce

1 Put the rice in a bowl and, using your fingers as a rake, rinse under cold running water to remove any dust. Drain the rice in a colander.

2 Soak the dried mushrooms in boiling water for 30 minutes, then drain and squeeze out any excess water. Remove and discard the stems and chop the caps into 5 mm (¼ inch) dice. Cut the snow peas (mange tout) into 1 cm (½ inch) pieces.

3 Place the sausages on a plate in a steamer. Cover and steam over simmering water in a wok for 10 minutes, then cut them into 1 cm (½ inch) pieces.

4 Heat a wok over medium heat, add the oil and heat until hot. Stir-fry (scramble-fry) the sausage until it is brown and the fat has melted out of it. Remove with a wire sieve or slotted spoon and drain. Pour the oil from the wok, leaving 1 tablespoon.

5 Reheat the reserved oil over high heat until very hot. Stir-fry (scramble-fry) the red onion until soft and transparent. Add the mushrooms and carrot and stir-fry for 1 minute, or until fragrant.

6 Put the mushroom mixture in a
clay pot, casserole dish or saucepan
and stir in the soy sauce, rice,
2 litres (2.1 US qt/1.75 UK qt)
stock (broth) or water and
¼ teaspoon salt. Bring to the boil,
then reduce the heat and simmer
very gently, stirring occasionally,
for 1¾–2 hours, or until it has a
porridge-like texture and the
rice is breaking up. If it is too
thick, add water and return to
the boil. Toss in the snow peas
(mange tout) and sausage,
cover and stand for 5 minutes
before serving.

CREAMY FISH SOUP

Preparation time:
10 minutes

Total cooking time:
35 minutes

Serves 4–6

INGREDIENTS

- ¼ teaspoon saffron threads
- 1 litre (1.1 US qt/1.75 UK pt) fish stock (broth)
- ½ cup (125 ml/4¼ fl oz) dry white wine
- 1 onion, finely chopped
- 1 small carrot, finely chopped
- 1 stick (rib) celery, chopped
- 1 bay leaf
- 45 g (1⅔ oz) butter
- 2 tablespoons plain (all-purpose) flour
- 300 g (10½ oz) skinless fish fillets (e.g. snapper, orange roughy, bream), in bite-sized pieces
- 1 cup (250 ml/8½ fl oz) cream
- 2 teaspoons chopped fresh chives, to garnish

1 In a small bowl, soak the saffron threads in 2 tablespoons boiling water.

2 Put the fish stock (broth), wine, onion, carrot, celery and bay leaf in a large saucepan and slowly bring to the boil. Cover and simmer for 20 minutes. Strain and discard the vegetables. Stir the saffron (with the liquid) into the hot stock (broth).

3 In a clean saucepan, melt the butter and stir in the flour for 2 minutes, or until pale and foaming. Remove from the heat and gradually stir in the fish stock (broth). Return to the heat and stir until the mixture boils and thickens.

4 Add the fish and simmer for 2 minutes, or until the fish is cooked. Stir in the cream and heat through without boiling. Season with salt and ground white pepper, to taste. Serve garnished with chives.

NOTE: Saffron threads are quite costly, but they add a subtle flavour and vivid yellow to food. The bright orange threads are sold in small glass jars or tiny plastic packets. Some people squeeze the threads after soaking, to release more colour into the water.

HARIRA

Preparation time:
15 minutes

Total cooking time:
2 hours 25 minutes

Serves 4

INGREDIENTS

- 2 tablespoons olive oil
- 2 small brown onions, chopped
- 2 large cloves garlic, crushed
- 500 g (1 lb 2 oz) lamb shoulder steaks, trimmed of excess fat and sinew, cut into small chunks
- 1½ teaspoons ground cumin
- 2 teaspoons paprika
- ½ teaspoon ground cloves
- 1 bay leaf
- 2 tablespoons tomato paste (tomato puree)
- 1 litre (1.1 US qt / 1.75 UK pt) beef stock (broth)
- 3 × 300 g (10½ oz) cans chickpeas (garbanzo beans), rinsed and drained
- 800 g (1 lb 12 oz) can diced good-quality tomatoes
- ½ cup (30 g / 1 oz) finely chopped fresh coriander (cilantro)
- fresh coriander (cilantro) leaves, extra, to garnish
- small black (ripe) olives, for serving

1. Heat the oil in a large heavy-based saucepan or stockpot, add the onion and garlic and cook for 5 minutes, or until softened. Add the meat, in batches, and cook over high heat until the meat is browned on all sides. Return all the meat to the pan.

2. Add the spices and bay leaf to the pan and cook until fragrant. Add the tomato paste (tomato puree) and cook for about 2 minutes, stirring constantly. Add the stock (broth) to the pan, stir well and bring to the boil.

3. Add the chickpeas (garbanzo beans), tomato and chopped coriander (cilantro) to the pan. Stir, then bring to the boil. Reduce the heat and simmer for 2 hours, or until the meat is tender. Stir occassionally. Season, to taste.

4. Serve garnished with coriander (cilantro) leaves and small black (ripe) olives. Can be served with toasted pitta bread drizzled with a little extra virgin olive oil.

GREEN PEA SOUP

Preparation time:
20 minutes + 2 hours
soaking

Total cooking time:
1 hour 40 minutes

Serves 4–6

INGREDIENTS

- 1½ cups (330 g/11⅔ oz) green split peas
- 2 tablespoons oil
- 1 medium onion, finely chopped
- 1 celery stick (rib), finely sliced
- 1 medium carrot, finely sliced
- 1 tablespoon ground cumin
- 1 tablespoon ground coriander
- 2 teaspoons grated fresh ginger (gingerroot)

- 5 cups (1.25 litres/1.3 US qt/ 1.1 UK qt) vegetable stock (broth)
- 2 cups (310 g/11 oz) frozen green peas
- salt and freshly ground black pepper
- 1 tablespoon chopped fresh mint
- 4 tablespoons plain yoghurt or sour cream

1 Soak the split peas in cold water for 2 hours. Drain peas well. Heat oil in a large heavy-based pan and add onion, celery and carrot. Cook over medium heat for 3 minutes, stirring occasionally, until soft but not browned. Stir in cumin, coriander and ginger (gingerroot), then cook for 1 minute.

2 Add split peas and stock (broth) to pan. Bring to the boil; reduce heat to low. Simmer, covered, for 1½ hours, stirring occasionally.

3 Add frozen peas to pan and stir to combine; set aside to cool. When cool, puree soup in batches in a blender or food processor until smooth. Return to pan, gently reheat. Season with salt and pepper and then stir in mint. Serve in bowls with a swirl of yoghurt or sour cream.

MANHATTAN-STYLE SEAFOOD CHOWDER

Preparation time:	**Total cooking time:**	**Serves** 4–6
30 minutes	30 minutes	

INGREDIENTS

- 60 g (2 oz) butter
- 3 rashers bacon, chopped
- 2 onions, chopped
- 2 cloves garlic, finely chopped
- 2 sticks (ribs) celery, sliced
- 3 potatoes, diced
- 1.25 litres (1.3 US qt/1.1 UK qt) fish or chicken stock (broth)
- 3 teaspoons chopped fresh thyme
- 12 raw large prawns (shrimp)

- 1 tablespoon tomato paste (tomato puree)
- 425 g (15 oz) can chopped tomatoes
- 375 g (13¼ oz) skinless white fish fillets (e.g. ling, cod, flake, hake), cut into bite-sized pieces
- 310 g (11 oz) can baby clams, undrained
- 2 tablespoons chopped fresh parsley
- grated orange rind, to garnish

1 Melt the butter in a large pan and cook the bacon, onion, garlic and celery over low heat, stirring occasionally, for 5 minutes, or until soft but not brown.

2 Add the potato, stock (broth) and thyme to the pan and bring to the boil. Reduce the heat and simmer, covered, for 15 minutes.

3 Meanwhile, peel the prawns (shrimp) and pull out the dark vein from each prawn back, starting at the head end. Add the tomato paste (tomato puree) and tomato to the pan, stir through and bring back to the boil. Add the fish pieces, prawns (shrimp) and clams with juice and simmer over low heat for 3 minutes. Season, to taste, and stir in the parsley. Serve garnished with the grated orange rind.

INDEX